EVERYDAY
battles

RISING ABOVE THE ADVERSARY'S SUBTLE SNARES

EVERYDAY
battles

BETTE S. MOLGARD

BOOKCRAFT
SALT LAKE CITY, UTAH

Library of Congress Catalog Card Number: 99-71854

ISBN 1-57008-656-7

First Printing, 1999

Printed in the United States of America

Contents

~
Everyday
Battles

Young Sister Chelsea Jones sits on the stand prior to giving her first talk in her new ward. Barely out of high school and just starting her college classes, she enjoys the opportunity to observe her fellow sisters while Bishop Johnson recites his familiar announcements. His voice takes a back seat as she spots sisters that might represent the future Chelsea, and she quietly daydreams of the possibilities.

Halfway back, to the left, she sees Michael and Alyson Smith. They are newlyweds and had been introduced in the Gospel Doctrine class as such the same week Chelsea had given her own introductions. Michael has his arm around Alyson and predictably, Alyson looks radiant.

Behind the Smiths sits the bishop's family. Sister Johnson balances a baby girl on one knee and hands a book to her next oldest child. Two sons and three other daughters complete the picture. "I wonder how she does it all," admires Chelsea as her gaze moves on down the bench.

She smiles as her eyes meet sweet Sister Jennings, who, Chelsea understands, was married to the stake patriarch before his death several years ago. Sister Jennings had made a special point to welcome Chelsea her first week in the ward. She had seen her Christlike countenance immediately, and it still quietly shines today.

Sister Jennings sits beside June Davis, a wonderfully vibrant single sister who has worked as an airline stewardess since her mission to France. "I wonder why she's not married," muses Chelsea. "Oooh, her job must be so exciting!"

Through the eyes of Chelsea Jones, these sisters' lives look so simple and happy. Bishop Johnson, on the other side of the stand, knows differently. He scans the same congregation while listening to Chelsea's talk and sees a more realistic picture.

Michael and Alyson Smith remind him of his own first weeks of marriage. He smiles to himself at his reflective thoughts. "Yes," thinks Bishop Johnson, "the everyday reality will set in soon. But if they hang on, they will find security, peace, and happiness beyond their fondest dreams." His thoughts quickly turn to his own family seated behind the young Smith couple. How he loves his wife, LaNae! His face softens as he watches her rock baby Sarah, now nestled comfortably on her shoulder. "A natural-born mother," he thinks; then he sighs as he remembers how hard LaNae is on herself. Just yesterday he had found her in tears as he walked through the door. Her explanation came between sobs, "I knew you would be in a hurry to eat the minute you came through the door so you could be on time to your temple recommend interviews. The baby started to cry, so I ran back to her crib as I asked Billy to hurry and set the table. Jared was having trouble with a puzzle and wanted me to help, so I called back out to Billy to make sure he was moving away from the television and setting the table. When I went out five minutes later, there he sat, still watching T.V. I was so frustrated that I lost my temper and gave him a loud Scotch blessing. Brother Taylor rang the doorbell right in the middle of my shouting. Now he knows what kind of wife you have. I'm supposed to be an example, and I try so hard, but I'm just not good enough. How can I be a bishop's wife when I can't even control my temper?" Bishop Johnson's comforting words had seemed to soothe her, but she had still appeared discouraged when he had visited with her during an early breakfast this morning.

His eyes naturally take the same path Chelsea's have taken,

and he notices Sister Jennings. His thoughts also mirror Chelsea's: "Sweet Sister Jennings. Surely she might have some words of wisdom for my disheartened wife," he thinks. Then remembering a recent temple recommend interview where Sister Jennings had shared some of her personal concerns including occasional loneliness, her fear of becoming a burden on her children as her health problems increased, and her desire to live to see her oldest son come back into the fold, he realizes she is not without her problems. Her problems are just different than LaNae's.

Different still are June Davis's problems, and those of newly divorced single mother Janet Jenkins. "No one is exempt," concludes the bishop, recalling the words of Sister Patricia T. Holland, who said:

> The perspective I have gained over these many years of listening to the worries of women is that no one woman or group of women—single, married, divorced, or widowed, homemakers or professional—has cornered the full market on concerns. There seems to be plenty of challenges to go around. And, I hasten to add, marvelous blessings as well. In this, too, we are united in our diversity. Every one of us does have privileges and blessings, and we do have fears and trials (*A Heritage of Faith: Talks Selected from the BYU Women's Conferences*, ed. Mary E. Stovall and Carol Cornwall Madsen [Salt Lake City: Deseret Book Co., 1988], pp. 14–15).

Yes, every sister in the Church finds herself fighting everyday battles. Whether single or married, young or old, we all fight the same battles against discouragement, fear, priority choices, addictions, gossip, and perfectionism. What many of us are not aware of, however, is that these familiar battles all originate as subtle snares of the adversary. Like a group relishing the aroma while walking past a bakery, we don't even realize that we have been deliberately distracted.

Why would Satan be so interested in distracting us? Women in general pose a serious threat to Satan's plan. His concern started with mother Eve. No sooner had Adam and Eve begun their life in the garden than Satan "sought also to beguile Eve, for he knew not the mind of God, wherefore he sought to destroy the world" (Moses 4:6). Why? Eve was the mother of all living. Through her would come every spirit that followed the Father's plan. Included in that seed would be Jesus Christ, whose Atonement would be the "keystone in the arch of the great plan which the Father had brought forth for the eternal life of His sons and daughters" (Gordon B. Hinckley, *Teachings of Gordon B. Hinckley* [Salt Lake City: Deseret Book Co., 1997], p. 30).

We, as Latter-day Saint women, continue to pose a disturbing threat to Satan and his armies. We have been placed on this earth to fulfill a specific role in the plan of salvation. No matter what our station in life, we have been placed in this time of all times, in our particular circumstances to fill the measure of our creation, which includes an individual mortal plan. Elder Neal A. Maxwell said, "It does no violence even to our frail human logic to observe that there cannot be a grand plan of salvation for all mankind, unless there is also a plan for each individual. The salvational sum will reflect all its parts" ("Meeting the Challenges of Today," *1978 Devotional Speeches of the Year* [Provo, UT: BYU Press, 1979], p. 153).

Our Savior and Heavenly Father need us all to carry out our individual plans. We each have something to give to the salvational sum. Our inspired Relief Society guidelines state that "every woman has been endowed by God with distinctive characteristics, gifts and talents in order that she may fulfill a specific mission in the eternal plan" (see Thomas S. Monson, "Move with Vision, Fueled by Faith," *Church News* [Salt Lake City: Deseret News Publishing Co.], 21 Mar. 1992). That specific mission makes each one of us a vital part of the salvational sum. First Corinthians Chapter 12 tells us, "And there are diversities of operations, but it is the same God which worketh all in all. . . . For as the body is one, and hath many members, and all the members of that one body, being many, are one body: so also is Christ. . . . For the body is not one member, but many. If the foot shall say, Because I am not the hand, I am not of the body; is it therefore not of the body? And if the ear shall say, Because I am not the eye, I am not of the body; is it therefore not of the body? If the whole body were an eye, where were the hearing? If the whole were hearing, where were the smelling? But now hath God set the members every one of them in the body, as it hath pleased him" (vv. 6, 12, 14–18).

If we didn't have our single sisters, our widows, our divorcees, our mothers, or our wives, we wouldn't have the whole body. Moreover, Satan is painfully aware of the eternal difference any one of our righteous sisters can make while carrying out her individual mission. Keep in mind, "Out of small things proceedeth that which is great" (D&C 64:33).

Let's take, for example, the problem Satan sees with allowing one righteous mother to raise five children free of his constant distractions. Her strength and testimony is passed on to subsequent generations. If each of those children had four children, and each of the subsequent generations did the same, look what happens to that small beginning: first generation: 20 children; second: 80 children; third: 320 children; fourth: 1280 children; fifth: 5120 children; sixth: 25,600 children; seventh: 102,400 children; eighth: 409,600 children; ninth: 1,638,400 children; tenth generation: 6,553,600 children! That doesn't count spouses, missionary converts brought into the Church (which also multiply exponentially), and people whose lives they touch in righteously living the gospel.

Mothers aren't his only threat. There is no limit to what any Latter-day Saint woman can do as she righteously fills the measure of her creation. What is the full eternal measure of a woman's creation? That depends on your viewpoint. Are you looking through Satan's tinted perception or through the clear, perfect lenses of the Savior's plan of happiness? Who are we? We are daughters of perfect parentage. Melvin J. Ballard explained: "No matter to what heights God has attained or may attain, he does not stand alone; for side by side with him, in all her glory, a glory like unto his, stands a companion, the Mother of his

children. For as we have a Father in heaven, so also we have a
Mother there, a glorified, exalted, enobled mother" (Bryant S.
Hinckley, *Sermons and Missionary Services of Melvin Joseph Bal-
lard* [Salt Lake City: Deseret Book Co., 1949], pp. 205–6).

We have the power to become like her, to stand side by side
with our companion as a glorified, exalted, enobled mother. That
statement doesn't eliminate any sister—old, young, widowed, or
divorced. Keeping an eternal vision will help us stay on the correct course throughout life. Ardeth G. Kapp shared her insight:

> We [because of our inability to have children] were alone
> with each other at a motel in St. George, Utah, one Thanksgiv-
> ing time when all our relatives were with their families. Early in
> the morning, I lay in bed thinking. I remember my heart crying
> out as I anticipated Christmas approaching. And although we
> could share in the joy and excitement of our nieces and nephews,
> it wasn't like having our own children with stockings to hang.
> The whole thing seemed to me to be unfair. I felt darkness and
> despondency settle over me, and I did what I had learned to do
> over the years. I got on my knees and prayed for insight.
>
> My answer came when I opened the scriptures to Doctrine
> and Covenants 88:67–68: "And if your eye be single to my glory
> [and remember, God's glory is to help 'to bring to pass the
> immortality and eternal life of man' (Moses 1:39)], your whole
> bodies shall be filled with light, and there shall be no darkness in
> you; and that body which is filled with light comprehendeth all
> things. Therefore, sanctify yourselves that your minds become
> single to God, and the days will come that ye shall see him; for
> he will unveil his face unto you, and it shall be in his own time,
> and in his own way, and according to his own will." . . .
>
> If I have any comforting message for others, it is this: Peace
> of mind comes from keeping an eternal perspective. Mother-
> hood, I believe, is a foreordained mission. For some, this glori-
> ous blessing may be delayed, but it will not be denied. Mother-
> hood is an eternal reality for all women who live righteously and
> accept the teachings of the gospel (*My Neighbor, My Sister, My
> Friend* [Salt Lake City: Deseret Book Co., 1990], pp. 127–28).

Keeping an eternal perspective as we head towards our glorious, ultimate goal is often difficult. Some women seem to be so much closer than others. How do we get there from here? We need to keep in mind that there are numerous pathways that will eventually merge into eternal life and exaltation.

Max's family has a cabin in Alpine, Wyoming. Floating down the Snake River is an experience that we enjoy multiple times each summer. It begins for some hardy folks in the late spring when the Tetons give their frigid water to the rising river. We prefer a warmer, less-treacherous float so we watch the crazy people for a month and then take our first trip of the season. By that time, the river is teeming with activity. Every ten seconds a group or individual pulls off the ramp at West Table Creek and begins their two-hour adventure. Everyone has a different plan which seems to depend on age, experience, and their choice of transportation. We now take a big gray rubber raft—a grand improvement over our floppy black raft of years gone by. Those who want to get soaked sit in the front and ride the bucking waves as they clutch the rope that serves as reins. Timid first-timers plant themselves in the middle and cower to the bottom of the boat when things get threatening. The more experienced strong ones straddle the sides and steer the boat with great forward and backward strokes of their paddles.

Someone has to take the truck from West Table Creek down to the take-out point at Sheep Gulch. A fun time filler for that person is to stop and hike down to the rocks that surround the intimidating set of rapids called "Lunchcounter" that immediately follow a thrilling near-waterfall named the "Great Kahuna." Watching the variations on the trip through those rapids is fascinating. Some boats skirt around the edge and miss most of the excitement. Those in kayaks hover on the top of the waves as they try to maintain balance and control with their double-bladed paddles. Teenagers shout with excitement as their invincible thinking carries them through in small inner tubes. Groups that don't realize the danger leave their people still straddling the sides and they can be catapulted off the side as the Great Kahuna garnishes another point. Their lifejacketed figures bob along in the churning rapids until they are hauled into their raft, picked up by another or remain a helpless victim of the powerful water. Tossed over and under they are powerless until they are spit out further downstream to calmer waters.

At the river's end, just before it feeds into the Palisades Reservoir, the river conquerors merge to the right. The ramp at Sheep Gulch is always alive with commercial vans dragging quadruple stacked raft trailers, and smaller private trucks and cars trying to reclaim the rafts. The hundreds who started at West Table Creek all stand triumphant enjoying the warming rays of the sun. Though each started and ended the same, there were hundreds of variations. Some ooze with excitement, some shiver with cold, and some feel grateful to have survived.

Likewise, our lives have hundreds of modifications. The river is wide and full of a myriad of possibilities that move us to the same glorious exaltation. With our eye on that goal, we present an awesome threat to the adversary's cause.

Picture with me the grand satanic council. In attendance are the leaders of the vast throng representing a third of the host of heaven (no, they probably didn't get out of all their meetings by following him). They meet to discuss a growing concern: that of their dealings with Latter-day Saint women. Let's listen in on their basic concerns:

"As you know, our experience has taught us that Latter-day Saint women don't run when we flash a major sin in front of them. The majority aren't tempted by immorality, theft, deceit, or the myriad of our other favorite 'capital S' sins. As soon as we try our usual tactics, the Holy Ghost sends up a bright yellow caution sign. This isn't the first time we have encountered this problem. We came upon it thousands of years ago with Moses."

And it came to pass that when Moses had said these words, behold, Satan came tempting him, saying: Moses, son of man, worship me.

And it came to pass that Moses looked upon Satan and said:

Who art thou? For behold, I am a son of God, in the similitude of his Only Begotten; and where is thy glory, that I should worship thee?

For behold, I could not look upon God, except his glory should come upon me, and I were transfigured before him. But I can look upon thee in the natural man. Is it not so, surely? (Moses 1:12–14).

"Moses had already felt the bright light of the Savior and could recognize the different feeling when he encountered our darkness. You may remember that we didn't make that same mistake in the Sacred Grove. We showed up before Joseph Smith had his vision, which, come to think of it, didn't work out that well either.

"Apparently, we need to be extremely subtle when working with Latter-day Saints. We need to use snares that they may not initially recognize as sins. Maybe they wouldn't necessarily ever be classified as sins; perhaps a diversion to distract them and waste their time would prove to be just as effective—especially if they never recognize the source of these distractions."

That cunning plan has been exceptionally successful. We have been blessed with many laborsaving devices, and Satan has filled our time with discouragement, fear, gossip, and addictions. We spend mindless hours watching television. We leave our families and run to work so we can buy more for ourselves and our children. We trade things of eternal importance for things of little importance. Our lives are so filled with the hustle of everyday living that we get to the end of the day exhausted, but no closer to reaching our spiritual goals. "No wonder that one of the adversary's favorite tactics among righteous women is busyness—getting us so preoccupied with the flurry of daily life that we fail to immerse ourselves in the gospel of Jesus Christ" (Sheri L. Dew, "We Are Not Alone," *Ensign*, Nov. 1998, p. 95).

What can we do to combat Satan's carefully set snares? How can we fight and ultimately triumph over our everyday battles? No matter what path we are taking, no matter what the battle,

the universal answer lies in ridding our lives of darkness and filling them with light. The presence of light is of utmost importance to children. You never hear of a child being scared of the
light, but fear of the dark is almost a given.

When I was seven years old, we moved into a small basement
apartment while we were building our home on the other side of
Brigham City, Utah. Quarters were exceedingly cramped. There
were six of us (seven when Grandpa visited) and only one bedroom. The living room was divided by a bookcase to allow us to
imagine the new bedroom for my older sister. I slept on the
couch. Rental storage units were not widely available then, so all
of our furniture and belongings from a fairly large home in Peo-
ria, Illinois, were "aesthetically" stacked along the walls making
the rooms even smaller.

One night, shortly after we had moved in, I woke up in the
middle of the night. Looking around the darkened room, to my
terror, I thought I saw a huge black bear standing only a few feet
away from the couch I was sleeping on—never mind the logistics
of a bear lumbering through the locked front door. I remember
lying as still as I could with the covers pulled up to allow only my
eyes to view the formidable scene. My heart pounded in fear, but
I didn't dare say anything, and hoped he wouldn't notice me. As
the minutes clicked by, the terror increased. Finally I couldn't
stifle my sobs and soon Daddy stumbled into my room, and
turned on the light as he asked what was the matter. The darkness of the room evaporated and with it the bear. All that was left
in the corner was a big box covered by a blanket.

Truth and light constantly vie against deception and darkness
for control of our minds while we are on this earth. The glorious
news is that darkness will never be as strong as light. Think of the
story of the young Joseph Smith as he knelt in the seclusion of
the Sacred Grove on that marvelous spring day in 1820. Having
decided to ask of God which church he should join, Joseph found
himself surrounded by the most awful darkness as soon as he
began to petition to the Lord for guidance. This terrible darkness
was so oppressive and powerful that the young prophet nearly

decided to abandon his purpose. But, thinking first to call upon God for deliverance, Joseph was soon surrounded by a magnificent light that descended from heaven and exiled the darkness.

As with the Prophet Joseph Smith's experience, when the murky shadows of the everyday battles of life cause us to call out in the dark, the Savior will come and with him bring light. He knows our battles. He understands our fear and discouragement. His is the ultimate empathy.

We all know the difference between empathy and sympathy. The difference was readily apparent to me when Max's father passed away. It was 1980 and we were living in Florida away from our families. My immediate family was still intact. I had never experienced the loss of a close family member. I'm great at sympathy, and that had been sufficient to buoy Max during difficult times that preceded that dark day in January. But then Max needed more than sympathy. He needed to talk to someone who "spoke the language" of close family loss. He called his area director, who had recently lost a son in a tragic accident. He knew how to speak the language of personal loss. Their conversation brought understanding and deep comfort.

As we go through life we learn different "languages." A single sister doesn't feel much comfort from speaking about her situation to a mother with a home full of children. They don't speak the same language. A young mother struggling with a teething baby won't get much sympathy and no empathy from her sixteen-year-old brother. He doesn't speak her young mother language. That young mother can give sympathy to a middle-aged mother struggling with a delinquent son, but a mother who has been through the same experience actually speaks the language and can offer so much more.

I watched as my daughter-in-law Anna went through labor and delivery when our granddaughter Meggan was born. The hours of bearing down pains seemed to go on forever to this outside observer who had traveled that path before. I was so caught up in the drama that my stomach muscles automatically contracted with each wave. I felt her distress. I knew the language.

Our Savior felt the pain of our everyday battles in the Garden of Gethsemane. He felt every fear, discouragement, every single hurt the adversary can throw at us. I don't know how he did it. I only know that he somehow individually felt and fought every single one of my battles, and every single one of your battles. He did it so that he would know exactly how to comfort and succor us. The Atonement allowed him to understand all of our languages:

> And he shall go forth, suffering pains and afflictions and temptations of every kind; and this that the word might be fulfilled which saith he will take upon him the pains and the sicknesses of his people.
>
> And he will take upon him death, that he may loose the bands of death which bind his people; and he will take upon him their infirmities, that his bowels may be filled with mercy, according to the flesh, that he may know according to the flesh how to succor his people according to their infirmities (Alma 7:11–12).

We are not alone. The chaos of the world will be stilled in our lives if we are following the plan our Father in Heaven and his Son have outlined for us. Their work is described in Moses 1:39: "For behold, this is my work and my glory—to bring to pass the immortality and eternal life of man." In other words, they both consecrate all of their time to bring us to them. We know who we are and where we are going. When our lives join hands with theirs, there is nothing we can't accomplish.

My earnest prayer is that this book will help to uncover the subtle snares the adversary uses to deceive and waste the precious time of Latter-day Saint women. With that knowledge, we will be able to banish the darkness and join hands with the whole body of Christ, that every sister might effectively live to fill the full measure of her creation.

Invite
the Light

$\mathcal{I}$ SHOULD HAVE PAID MORE attention. It was written in black and white the week after Patriarch H. Eugene Perry vocalized my individual blessing from Heavenly Father. I know now how well Father knew me that day, and more important, he knew what I would be like as a teenager, a newlywed, a parent, and a grandmother, for he could see my future. In my case, and for many like me, one sentence from my patriarchal blessing says it all: "Satan will see that trials and obstacles are placed in your path to discourage you in the work of the Lord."

The "D" word has been my nemesis. Discouragement creeps in during low ebbs and builds inside until it snuffs out much that is good. I have been aware of the havoc discouragement brings to my life but only recently did I become aware of the other important part of the warning contained in my patriarchal blessing: the source of my discouragement is Satan. The plans of that grand satanic council have been so successful that many women, like myself, striving with all of their hearts to keep all of the commandments and covenants fail to recognize the source of their despondency.

Our youngest son, McKay, seemed to have come with "trouble" stamped on his forehead. If he didn't, it was indelibly marked there during his second year. In a two-day period he poured glue on our brand new computer keys (he thought they were loose and he was fixing them for me); filled my dryer with flour (no explanation); and tried to flush the baby Jesus figurine from our hand-carved nativity set that we'd bought in Bethlehem down the toilet. With that final rescue, we should have suspected the source of our next problem.

Our toilet was plugged and wouldn't flush. My husband, Max, plunged it and plunged it until he broke out in a sweat. He quite patiently (I thought) plunged more the next day and several times Sunday. We didn't have the extra money that would pay for a plumber's visit. After one final heroic attempt, Max acknowledged defeat and asked me to call in the pros. An hour after their arrival, I heard the water slurp and knew they had been more successful than my husband. Looking at the bill, I spied the words, "Nine potatoes removed." No wonder it wouldn't flush! Once I knew the source of the problem, my bucket of potatoes was put out of McKay's reach and nothing else (except all of his training pants several months later) was ever flushed. The problem was solved once we knew the source.

We cannot solve the sometimes overwhelming problem of discouragement without realizing where it comes from. A young elder received wise counsel from his stake president just before he left on his mission: "Discouragement comes from Satan. Heavenly Father would never want us to feel let down or sad, but happy, enthusiastic and optimistic" (*Church News* [Salt Lake City: Deseret News Publishing Company], Oct. 21, 1995).

Joseph Fielding McConkie adds to our knowledge of Satan's realm when he writes:

> The Spirit of the Lord and all doctrines that trace to it must edify. The principles of salvation have no kinship with hopelessness, depression, or grief. They are not dark, cold, or unfeeling. Truth always sustains the idea of a just and merciful God. If a principle does not lift, encourage, inspire, or edify it certainly does not come from God and cannot be considered doctrine. Perhaps the two most often used words to describe the presence

of the Holy Ghost are "peace" and "joy." In scripture the gospel is often referred to as "glad tidings," or "glad tidings of great joy" (Mosiah 3:3; Alma 13:22; D&C 31:3; 128:19). Good doctrine will always carry a positive and uplifting spirit (*Answers: Straightforward Answers to Tough Gospel Questions* [Salt Lake City: Deseret Book Co., 1998], p. 13).

Satan is the source; therefore we automatically know the quality of his message. The scriptures warn us, "Satan seeketh to turn their hearts away from the truth" (D&C 78:10). Oliver Wendell Holmes once said, "Sin has many tools, but a lie is the handle which fits them all" (see Obert C. Tanner, *Christ's Ideals for Living* [Salt Lake City: Deseret Sunday School Union Board, 1955], p. 96). And Satan is the father of lies (see John 8:44). Joseph F. Smith explained:

> Let it not be forgotten that the evil one has great power in the earth, and that by every possible means he seeks to darken the minds of men, and then offers them falsehood and deception in the guise of truth. Satan is a skilful imitator, and as genuine gospel truth is given the world in ever-increasing abundance, so he spreads the counterfeit coin of false doctrine. Beware of his spurious currency, it will purchase for you nothing but disappointment, misery and spiritual death. The "father of lies" he has been called, and such an adept has he become, through the ages of practice in his nefarious work, that were it possible he would deceive the very elect (*Gospel Doctrine* [Salt Lake City: Deseret Book Co., 1939], p. 376).

We are the very elect, and if we aren't constantly vigilant, we will believe the lies and waste precious time that could be spent in our growth towards truth and righteousness.

I watch home movies from time to time. The happy memories of my life spring back into focus as I peruse each phase. I had always been the very smallest in every class at elementary school. Every year at class picture time, we would line up from tallest to shortest and I would automatically head to the end of the line. It didn't bother me and my class pictures show a smiling blonde on the end of the front row . . . every year. I wasn't just short either. I was little through and through.

Then in my seventh grade year I, along with the rest of the seventh grade girls, "blossomed" into womanhood. I happened to blossom more rapidly than most and found my poor mother trying desperately to keep up with the dress code of skirt lengths as I grew seven inches that year. Nothing really fit for long. And I proudly stood my tallest as Dad measured me against the last mark on the wall.

One fateful day I was wearing some cotton black and turquoise plaid shorts that were on their final day of wear. Cotton doesn't stretch and my female curves had come to the limit of those shorts and they were no longer comfortable. One of the most popular girls in the junior high rounded the aisle in J.C. Penney and spotted me. "Bette," she said in amazement, "you're so much bigger than the last time I saw you!"

Cindy could just as easily have meant my height, but in my tight plaid shorts I automatically concluded that she thought I was fat. Looking at the upheaval that thought caused, I firmly believe Satan was the source. He planted that seed and over the years it grew and grew until that thought and the discouragement that it brought overwhelmed me.

Was I fat? Hardly. By the time I made the drill team at Box Elder High School, I was a "whopping" 125 pounds on my five-foot-three-inch frame. But the other girls on the drill team seemed to weigh 98 pounds. They were all different heights and I was one of the shortest, which meant that many of them probably weighed more than I did. But once a month the announcement, "Weigh-ins will be this Friday," ruined my life. Weigh-ins consisted of three girls, who made up the drill team presidency, and the advisor watching as each girl stood on the scale. I would make myself sick anticipating weigh-ins and then would exacerbate the problem trying to solve it in less than a week. Mom took "water pills" every once in a while and I discovered that if I took one or two of those the day before and the day of weigh-ins, I would weigh a lot less. (Never mind the stupidity of taking a water pill while working as a lifeguard at the outdoor city swimming pool.) I figured it was all worth it. I quietly endured the step on the scale and vowed to lose those ten pounds honestly by the next weigh-in.

The major problem was that those thoughts of despair and discouragement because of my weight didn't just come into my thoughts at weigh-in time. I brooded over my inflated size before I went to sleep at night and thought about it first thing the following morning. I thought about it throughout the day as I condemned myself then and for years to come.

Now I look at the pictures of my little frame, one that looks very close to the size of everyone else on the drill team, and know how carefully Satan duped me. It is no exaggeration when I admit I wasted thousands and thousands of hours entertaining his lie. What righteous works could I have done with those hours? My experience highlights Spencer J. Condie's thoughts: "Discouragement and its fellow travelers of depression, despair, and hopelessness are much like the proverbial rocking chair: they keep us busily occupied, but they do not take us anywhere" ("Agency: The Gift of Choices," *Ensign*, Sept. 1995, p. 20).

As I've written this chapter my thoughts have been tremendously reinforced. Satan and his armies are on a rampage, using lies to discourage the elect. Our oldest daughter, now twenty-four years old, never gave us problems while she was growing up. One time, she thought she was in big trouble. She sluffed school with a group of her friends and went to Temple Square in Salt Lake City. It wasn't a problem with us; in fact we were silently thrilled that she had "almost" done something normal. But she took off her Young Womanhood Recognition medallion for a month in penance. She continues to be a righteous daughter. Her comment to me this week was: "My faith is at a low point right now. Maybe I don't deserve to be blessed." Good job, Satan.

An attractive, talented friend of mine has chosen to stay home and raise six spiritual and intellectual leaders. She is married to a fine priesthood holder and lives in a beautiful home. Her oldest daughter married in the temple. Her oldest son is filling out his mission papers. She should be reveling in deserved praise, but her comment told me how convincing Satan is: "I just don't know if I'm doing anything of worth." Nothing could be further from the truth.

Life is full of adversity, and the lows it creates make us prime targets to Satan's voice. Libby Knapp shared her story in the March 1991 *Ensign*. She was married, full of life and energy, and expecting her first child when a progressive chronic disease began to attack her body. She shares what she has learned in the past nine years:

> The adversary works with all his might to convince me that losing some abilities lessens my individual worth. Why, even the phrase "What's wrong with me?" has negative implications.
> . . . Denial, anger, apathy, and depression are all normal reactions to losing one's health. I still have periods when I mourn the loss of my abilities—and I probably always will. It does not mean I am less valiant because I have these feelings. But it *is* a mistake to turn from the Lord, for he can offer comfort and sustenance ("Living with Chronic Illness," *Ensign*, Mar. 1991, pp. 51–53).

Sister Knapp found that counseling with the Lord in prayer, turning to the scriptures, finding ways to serve, and maintaining a hopeful attitude enables her to find joy in a very difficult situation. I can personally testify that variations in health, particularly chronic ailments, open the easy-access door to Satan's discouraging whisperings.

We will all pass through difficult times in our lives when we know Satan and his followers have set up camp in our home. Thankfully, there will be other times when we are so full of the Spirit that we feel like we have a steel shield of protection against the adversary. We attended an area conference in Florida in 1979. The entire United States was alive with debates concerning the Equal Rights Amendment. Members of the Church were especially targeted as opponents that needed to rethink their position. President Spencer W. Kimball and Elder LeGrand Richards spoke at the conference and filled our spiritual cups to overflowing. For many in attendance it was a chance in a lifetime to be in the presence of a prophet and an apostle and we all basked in the glow of the Spirit. The closing song was "God Be with You Till We Meet Again." We had taken our seven-year-old daughter, Michelle, with us. She wore a white dress and stood on the bench during the song waving her white hanky at President Kimball, who waved his hanky at the mass of humanity waving back. The hankies weren't just for waving. The overflowing of our spiritual cups was somehow connected to our eyes, and tears were flowing. When the last notes of the closing song faded, everyone sat down except Michelle, who hesitated and gave President Kimball one last wave of her hanky. Somehow, she caught his eye and he looked right at her and gave her a personal smile and wave. I'll never forget her face. "He waved at just me!" she said, glowing as she sat down and listened to the closing prayer.

Against that background, the Equal Rights Amendment folks chose to make a valiant but totally ineffective stand. Hundreds of dollars were spent securing an airplane to fly over the conference center immediately following our meeting. The gigantic banner pulled behind the plane flipped in a breeze that I'm positive was the only resulting ripple felt that day. Nothing could have penetrated our spiritual barrier.

Spiritual highs, however, are not the norm. Even when we're living a life filled with doing the right things, mortality and the world can get in our way giving Satan's army easy access.

Our daughter-in-law Anna is oozing with talent. She attended and graduated from Brigham Young University with a full scholarship and numerous honors in the music department. A Sterling Scholar from high school, her feelings of worth were strongly connected to scholarly accolades. Many people actively encouraged her to continue her education, counting on a promising contribution to the world of music.

Meggan Marie was born shortly after Anna's graduation.

Anna and Max Jr. have been blessed because of their unmoveable decision to have Anna stay home and be Meggan's full-time mom. As much as Anna loves Meggan, the difficulty of balancing the checkbook, and the mundane repetition of diapers, laundry, nursing, and cleaning at times allow discouraging whisperings of "If you were working, things would be easier financially; you're not using your talents in the most effective way. For this you studied so hard?!" Inquiries regarding her employment always make her want to defend her "non-working" position even though she knows her work at home is harder and infinitely more important than anything she could be doing at a job. The inter- mittent reinforcers of doing what you know you should be doing give Satan ample time to flash temptations offering immediate rewards.

Single sisters have heard President Hinckley say, "Our Father in Heaven reserves for them every promised blessing" (see *Church News,* 13 Apr. 1991); but the years are long. Many sisters without children long for their desired blessing. Many with chil- dren find that the road can be treacherous and that no matter how righteous the parents, some children choose to stray. Sister missionaries often find that their years of service have great highs and scraping lows. Discouragement caution signs are posted on all these roads taken by Latter-day Saint sisters. No matter how attractive life looks in someone else's shoes, each has its advan- tage and disadvantage.

President Gordon B. Hinckley said:

> Anyone who imagines that bliss is normal is going to waste a lot of time running around shouting that he's been robbed. The fact is that most putts don't drop, most beef is tough, most children grow up to be just people, most successful marriages require a high degree of mutual toleration, most jobs are more often dull than otherwise. Life is like an old time rail journey . . . delays, sidetracks, smoke, dust, cinders, and jolts, interspersed only occasionally by beautiful vistas, and thrilling bursts of speed. The trick is to thank the Lord for letting you have the

ride (Address to Religious Educators, Temple Square Assembly Hall, Sept. 1980).

We, as members of his Church, are very grateful for the beautiful vistas. We know the glorious blessings that are ours. I can't even imagine the ride without the knowledge of the gospel of Jesus Christ. He is my Savior and the Holy Ghost is my guide through this "old time rail journey." A diligent awareness of the presence of our uninvited hitchhiker through the delays, sidetracks, and jolts is the first step in conquering Satan's discouragement.

In our little community, young boys start playing T-ball when they are six. We chuckle when we think about our son's first year. We would be watching the boy at bat swinging desperately, trying to knock the ball off the tee and then we'd glance in the outfield to see the center fielder sitting in the grass totally oblivious to the drama at home plate. He could get hit on the head with the ball and not have a clue where it came from. Worse yet, the ball could drop right beside him and he would likely remain oblivious and continue picking dandelions.

Consider that same team after several years of practice. The tee is gone. They know that the "source" of the ball is the pitcher and that he stands in the middle of the field on a mound of dirt. They can keep a watchful eye in the right direction and when they recognize a good pitch, they can smack the ball clean out of the park.

In a like manner, we can recognize the source of those degrading, disheartening, discouraging thoughts. Before that recognition, we were obliviously picking the dandelions, so caught up with the business of life that Satan could quietly plant his destructive seeds just beyond our field of vision. Now our vision has expanded. We must diligently guard against the adversary or he will sow seeds of tragic proportions. Speaking about the seeds of our thoughts, Hugh B. Brown said:

> Our Father is kind and loving and forgiving, but there is an inexorable law which has not been repealed. It is the law of the harvest: "As ye sow, so shall ye reap" (Galatians 6:7). We cannot

sow thistles and reap figs, nor plant thorns and harvest grapes. But when we have had enough of thistles and thorns, we may have the grapes and the figs if we are willing to pay the price—and they cost less. While ours is a world governed by rigid and unwavering law, man has free agency, he may choose to obey or disobey the law, but he must of course abide the consequences of his choice (Conference Report, Apr. 1955, p. 81).

Our free agency allows us to choose what we plant. If we choose to plant the weeds of discouragement and cultivate those weeds, they can multiply and replenish our despondent thoughts. We recently had a discussion with a son who didn't think it was right that we made him go to church every Sunday. His opinion: "If I don't go, you take away privileges. That's not free agency!"

Elaine Cannon shared a humorous story explaining the two parts included in every decision:

> A good man had been given the assignment in his ward of arranging the Boy Scout banquet. He had worked hard, made his choices, and carried them through. The tables were set, the food was in the pot, and the hour was drawing nigh.
>
> His wife came over early to check things out. Everything seemed in order, but it looked mighty colorless to her trained eye. She turned to him and said, "Okay, Honey, but what are you going to use for the centerpieces?"
>
> Surprised, he looked at the stark setting and considered the matter gravely for a moment. Then, in the full agency of his manhood, he replied, "Butter—squares of butter!"
>
> Now that is what you might call freedom of choice—agency. . . . I must add that should we happen to choose butter for the centerpiece, we can't expect compliments on the decor. We have our free agency, but we also have to accept the consequences of our choices.
>
> . . . Translated into simple idiom that means that if you pick up one end of a stick, you pick up the other. When you pick a path, you choose the place it leads to ("Agency and Account-ability," *Ensign,* Nov. 1983, p. 88).

If we choose to allow discouraging thoughts to linger in our minds, we choose to be discouraged. Is discouragement really a *choice*? I recently heard a woman tell about her internment in Auschwitz. As her mother was going to the gas chambers, she told her daughter, "Remember, they can take away everything but your thoughts. You have total control over what you think." This woman, now a doctor devoted to helping others, testified that we truly do have control, even in the worst of all situations.

But many of us have given that control over to Satan. Hugh W. Nibley told about Satan's power when he said: "How does Satan get that power? This is an interesting thing. Are the poor people just victimized by Satan? Satan is a ravening lion who goes along seeking those whom he may destroy, and they become his helpless victims. Don't fool yourself . . . He won't have power unless you yield yourself up to him" (*Teachings of the Book of Mormon—Semester 1: Transcripts of Lectures Presented to an Honors Book of Mormon Class at Brigham Young University, 1988–1990* [Provo, UT: FARMS, 1993], p. 314).

Moses 4:4 tells us: "And he became Satan, yea, even the devil, the father of all lies, to deceive and to blind men, and to lead them captive at his will, even as many as would not hearken unto my voice." When we give those lies space, we are "captive at his will." We choose to fill our minutes, hours, days, and, tragically, even years with those weeds of thought. What righteous progress could we have made? What service in the kingdom did we miss? Discouraged women in the Church tend to wallow in the mire and think, "That's life." The truth is, we have chosen to listen to Satan; we do have control over what we let stay in our minds and we can knock those thoughts "clean out of the ball park." Remember, Satan is a slow learner, but he eventually does learn what is no longer effective. When discouraging thoughts come into your mind, don't let them linger for a moment. You can say as Moses did, "Get thee hence, Satan; deceive me not" (Moses 1:16).

We read in Genesis that in the beginning, the "earth was without form, and void; and darkness was upon the face of the deep. And the Spirit of God moved upon the face of the waters. And God said, Let there be light: and there was light. And God saw the light, that it was good: and God divided the light from the darkness" (Genesis 1:2–4).

The light has been divided from the darkness ever since. Its division is figuratively shown in the day and the night. It is vitally important that we understand that the result of harboring discouragement is darkness in our minds; and that light can banish it. Stirling W. Sill taught:

> One of our most urgent present-day needs is to houseclean our thinking. Because two opposite thoughts cannot co-exist in the mind at the same moment, the best way to get rid of undesirable thoughts is by antedoting them with good. The best way to get darkness out of a room is to fill it with light. The best way to kill the negative is to cultivate the positive, and the best way to improve our lives is to improve our thoughts (Conference Report, Oct. 1959, p. 103).

We can find parallel feelings and a promised solution in the biblical account of Moses and the vast throng of the children of Israel wandering in the wilderness: "And they journeyed from mount Hor by the way of the Red sea, to compass the land of Edom: and the soul of the people was much *discouraged* because of the way" (Numbers 21:4, emphasis added).

The Savior told them how to overcome those difficult times: "When thou art in tribulation, and all these things are come upon thee, *even in the latter days,* if thou turn to the LORD thy God, and shalt be obedient unto his voice; (for the LORD thy God is a merciful God;) he will not forsake thee" (Deuteronomy 4:30–31, emphasis added).

We know the father of all lies is the source of darkness and discouragement. We also know the source of truth and light. Our Savior said, "I am the light, and the life, and the truth of the world" (Ether 4:12).

His reassuring light is so readily available to us. Brother

Robert Arnold served as a mission president in South America and at times he and his wife, Gwenda, have taken the opportunity to return as tour guides. During a recent tour the group went to a "church" devoted to pagan worship. A wooden idol carved in the form of a man was given cigarettes and alcohol as offerings. A young girl brought her sick baby to request the idol to heal it.

That girl haunts me. I try to imagine myself with a sick baby knowing nothing about the gospel of Jesus Christ. I don't know about prayer, faith, the priesthood, or the comfort of the fellowship of my brothers and sisters. The only hope I have is to take my baby to a slab of wood and hope that it is accepting of my offerings.

Those thoughts humble me with overwhelming gratitude. We have been blessed with so much—everything. No matter what our circumstances, no matter how difficult the way, we know where we are heading and where to turn to feel the understanding arms of our Savior enfold us. His understanding is universal and all encompassing.

Richard Norby, a seminary teacher in Tooele, Utah, recently taught that we should try asking a six-year-old Latter-day Saint child who her favorite person and what her favorite song are. Invariably she will choose Jesus, Mom, or a Primary teacher and a Primary song. When you ask a teenager or adult what her favorites are, you get a whole variety of responses, many times not desirable choices. Why? Because the six-year-old is always turned towards the source of light. Satan has no power over her. But a teenager or adult may be turned either direction, towards the light or the shadows.

Whenever you see a picture of or think of the Savior, you never see his back. His arms are always outstretched towards us, no matter where we move. If we are in a shadow, it must be we who moved or put something between us and the Savior.

Our challenge as women in the Church is to stay out of the shadows, keeping ourselves fully turned towards the light. Our hurry-scurry life easily lends itself to allowing walls to be built between us and the Savior. They aren't necessarily walls that we have built. They are more likely walls that build up while we're busy taking care of business elsewhere.

Banish the darkness from your mind and let your Savior fill it with light. Pray *before* you read your scriptures and feel the Lord fill your mind with the light of understanding. Listen to the whisperings of the Spirit, then act on those promptings. Pray *before* you go to the temple, then bask in the flood of light that will fill your mind and spirit. The strength of even a small piece of that light is able to lock out discouragement. Darkness cannot tolerate light.

Faith: The Great Replacement for Fear

OUR SON MAX JR. WAS BORN with a horrendous singing voice. He tried out for the high school musical his freshman year and didn't even hit one note correctly. Not to be discouraged, he took four years of voice lessons and eventually became the lead for the school musical his senior year.

His example gave me a boost of encouragement. I had always thought a beautiful voice was a talent brought from the premortal existence; something a person would be born with or without. I figured either I hadn't practiced before my sojourn on earth, or the practicing didn't do me any good. Although I could carry a tune, my voice was nothing to brag about and I quietly enjoyed singing within the walls of my own home. A bad experience twenty years before began a lifetime of extremely shy singing around others. Sitting in church, sharing a hymnbook, my whispery singing guaranteed that others wouldn't ever be able to criticize my voice. I had secretly concluded that my only hope for a beautiful singing voice lay in the resurrection. I reasoned that when my turn came, perhaps I would have earned the right to two requests beyond the normal blessing of a perfect body: that I could have two inches added to my legs between my hips and my knees (so that I could sit on a couch like a normal person) and that I could be granted a beautiful singing voice (with the voice being the top priority).

But Max Jr.'s voice teacher, Jean Poyer, presented another possibility. She explained that the voice is a musical instrument. With proper training (knowing where to put the air, how to hold your mouth, controlling your diaphragm, etc.) most anyone can be taught to sing. I could have a fine singing voice before the resurrection. The thought intrigued me, then excited me, and finally prompted me to give Jean a call. My lesson was set for the following Tuesday afternoon.

My initial excitement soon merged with dread. How did I think I could learn to sing when I couldn't bring myself to let someone sitting next to me in a large choir hear my voice? How could I possibly take voice lessons? We're not talking typical insecure trepidation. We're talking about nights up, heart beat in the throat, churning stomach terror. The thought of singing all alone in front of Jean petrified me. But it didn't erase my genuine desire to sing. That desire propelled me to Jean's home that Tuesday afternoon, where I whisper-sang through the lesson accompanied by Jean's patient encouragement.

Over the next several years my confidence with Jean increased. I could tell my voice was getting better, in fact some lessons I went home downright excited. But I still didn't share my voice with anyone else. If Jean's phone rang during my lesson, if her daughter Teri came within sight, or if a repairman came to her house, the lesson was over. My practice times at home were private, between me and our Chihuahua, Echo (who chimed right in if I didn't put him outside).

Four years into lessons, Jean was encouraging me to sing a solo. As far as I was concerned this was not within the realm of possibility. It was brought up and vetoed several times that year. That summer, Jean was facing serious back surgery. Her worst-case scenario of the outcome caused her to nonchalantly announce during one lesson, "I would like you to sing 'Thanks for the Music' at my funeral. I really do love the way you sing that."

Call it sympathy or temporary insanity, but I made a promise that day that would teach me to carefully think before I spoke, "I'm not going to sing at your funeral . . . you'll be just fine and I need lessons for many years to come. But I'll sing whatever you want me to sing, wherever you want me to sing on your birthday in January. Just don't ask me to sing at your funeral!"

January was months, almost half a year away. It seemed like a safe bet. Months passed. Jean came out of her surgery just fine and my lessons resumed in September. I had not forgotten my promise, but was not going to bring it up myself. Unfortunately, Jean also remembered. The closer we got to her birthday, the more fear brewed in me until it was fairly bubbling over the week before my debut. It seemed awfully silly. I can easily speak to hundreds. I can play the piano no matter who is listening. I guess we all have something we fear and singing in public happened to be my "thing." About a week before my promised solo was to take place, knowing that I couldn't go back on my promise and knowing that I couldn't sing "Thanks for the Music" for Jean's sacrament meeting, I was totally beside myself. One day I was biting my fingernails and pondering my frightening mess when a thought from a talk my husband gave several months before popped into my mind : "The opposite of fear is faith. The two cannot exist together." I pondered, then savored those words. President Gordon B. Hinckley described fear thus:

> Who among us can say that he or she has not felt fear? I know of no one who has been entirely spared. Some, of course, experience fear to a greater degree than do others. Some are able to rise above it quickly, but others are trapped and pulled down by it and even driven to defeat. We suffer from the fear of ridicule, the fear of failure, the fear of loneliness, the fear of ignorance. Some fear the present, some the future. Some carry the burden of sin and would give almost anything to unshackle themselves from those burdens but fear to change their lives. Let us recognize that fear comes not of God, but rather that this gnawing, destructive element comes from the adversary of truth

and righteousness. Fear is the antithesis of faith. It is corrosive in its effects, even deadly.

"For God hath not given us the spirit of fear; but of power, and of love, and of a sound mind" ("God Hath Not Given Us the Spirit of Fear," *Ensign*, Oct. 1984, p. 2).

Armed with this new idea I decided to conduct my own experiment. As a Latter-day Saint woman, I have been blessed with numerous faith-promoting experiences. I recognize the fuzzy warmth of faith and know that feeling cannot be duplicated or counterfeited by Satan. I have absolute confidence in my Father in Heaven, in his Son, my Savior, Jesus Christ, and in the prophets that speak for them. That confidence, or faith, did seem to contradict my fears. I remembered my fear, then felt my faith. It was true. When one feeling was in my heart, the other feeling departed. Faith, fear, fear, faith . . . the two battled back and forth until I discovered that faith was by far the stronger and could easily override the other. Using that concept I confidently sang my solo in the Little Mountain Ward sacrament meeting. That was a momentous occasion for me because I discovered some of the principles of faith that I have used over and over again.

Before explaining those principles of faith, I want to compare principles to trivia. They are worlds apart but get thrown together into the mishmash that so often becomes our personal study and public instruction. Trivia is information that is nice to know but is not important in forming a basis of our gospel knowledge. One of our favorite games to play is "Jots and Tittles," a Latter-day Saint version of Trivial Pursuit. Such questions as, "What does the Chaldean term Rhleenos mean?" (hieroglyphics); or "The 1835 edition of what measured only two and three-quarters inches by four and one-half inches?" (the first Church hymnbook) stump even the best of us. You might say, "Who cares?" That's exactly the point. Being able to answer trivia questions will never get us to the celestial kingdom. But jots and tittles very often clutter our Sunday School lessons, sacrament meetings and personal gospel study. We should be dwelling on principles. Principles are truths that never change no matter how much the world changes or how much time goes by. For example, King Benjamin taught, "wickedness never was happiness" (see Alma 41:10). That principle is true. It was true for Adam and Eve. It will be true throughout eternity. Watching for principles while studying the scriptures, preparing for a lesson or a talk, and teaching our children can be a glorious experience.

With that in mind, what eternal truths are principles of faith? My experience has taught me two important principles:

1. "True faith always moves its possessor to some kind of physical and mental action" (LDS Bible Dictionary, s.v. "Faith"). I used to think that faith was belief in something. That was only partially correct. James 2:19 set me straight: "Thou believest that there is one God; thou doest well: the devils also believe, and tremble." Believing in Christ and his power isn't impressive at all. Even Satan believes and look how far that gets him! Faith must be coupled with action.

2. Action will bring power beyond your natural ability. I liken it to a stick of dynamite representing power. That power can sit for eons of time unless someone uses action that will light the fuse—only then is the power accessed.

These principles of faith can be enlarged by two other principles I discovered that are related to fear:

1. The opposite of fear is faith.

2. Fear and faith cannot coexist. President Hinckley said fear comes from Satan. Faith comes as a gift of the Spirit from our Father in Heaven. Heavenly powers are always stronger than demonic powers. Therefore, faith is guaranteed to lock out fear.

Fear is in Satan's realm but, without that understanding, some Latter-day Saint sisters live in that realm. Single sisters may be full of fear that they will never meet their eternal mate. Married sisters may be full of fear because their children have strayed. Older sisters may fear illness or death. Whatever the fear, small or overwhelming, the principles of faith will lock out that key to Satan's access.

Our oldest son, Max Jr., and Anna Mohlman had been best friends since before Anna was old enough to date. She helped him pick out his tuxedo for the junior prom. I thought that was a little odd since she wasn't his date. When I commented on it, Max Jr. looked at me with a puzzled expression and said, "Mom, Anna's my friend like Brett is."

As the years went by, Anna became more than a buddy. By the time Max Jr. was ready to leave on his mission, we considered her part of our family. Many fears circled about concerning their future relationship, but Max Jr. seemed totally devoid of fear. One of his final comments before he left said it all: "You can't tell me that if I'm supposed to marry Anna, that chance will be taken away from me because I'm going to serve a mission. The Lord doesn't work that way. If Anna is to be my eternal companion, she won't get married while I'm gone."

In total faith he left on his mission and served righteously. That action brought him the promised power beyond his own ability. Two examples will reinforce the principle. On February 14, 1994, he wrote:

> Our bike helmets got stolen. They tried to steal our bikes, but they were luckily locked up pretty solidly. Elder Bird's bike tire got a flat. We were walking our bikes to a gas station to get air in the tire and get a bike patch kit. Luckily, one of the three Nephites stopped and helped us out. I seriously doubt it was one of the three Nephites, but check this story out. We were walking our bikes and a guy pulled over and said, "Do you want a new bike tube?" Thinking he was trying to sell us something or maybe he was crazy, we told him we would just fix this one. He reached in his back seat, pulled out a brand new, just the right size bike tube and gave it to Elder Bird. We asked him if he was a member. He said he was but he didn't have a set ward that he went to. We asked his name and he said, "Job" and left. It was pretty crazy. But pretty cool that we got a new bike tube.

> Love Y'all, Max

We knew someone was watching over our missionary but downtown Atlanta, Georgia, can be a dangerous place. Here is a letter we received dated March 14, 1994:

Hey Kenny & Dad, but not Mom,

Check this out . . . I got mugged! It was so cool! We were out tracting and walked back to our bikes to ride to our next appointment. When we got to our bikes, someone had flattened Elder Taylor's bike tire, so we had to walk our bikes home. It had just started to get dark and we were in a good neighborhood so we weren't very worried. As we were walking down the street a car pulled up beside us and a guy jumped out of the back seat and said, "The party's over gentlemen." As we turned, we saw a nice shiny revolver in his hand. I especially noticed it was pointed at me! He said, "I'll give you fifteen seconds and then I'm shooting and there had better be money in my hand!" Then he started counting. He was counting pretty quick also. He got to thirteen before he got the $5.02 we had on us. They really weren't too impressed, but they didn't have much time, since cars were going up and down the street. The interesting thing is that I've never had any money on me. That day was the first day I've ever had any money. For some reason I slipped a couple of dollars in my pocket, not thinking. Probably pretty wise and lucky (more than luck) that I had some money. I don't think our mugger would have been too impressed with 2 pennies. Satan knows he has to try to scare us somehow. He tries hard to keep us from doing the work, but he's out of luck.

Dad, it's up to you whether you share this with Mom or not. I truly am watched over and protected. Even in that situation there was no fear, because of the safety and feelings the spirit gave me. It's up to you. Just don't let her get on the next plane to Georgia. I'm more than fine.

Love ya, Your Elder

I didn't get on the first plane to Atlanta; in fact, that letter had the opposite effect. It totally erased all my fears regarding his

safety. I knew our Father's servants go forth armed with his
power and angels truly have charge over them (see D&C
109:22). As long as he remained faithful, the only way he would
be harmed would be for the Lord's purposes. Max Jr.'s faith had
been coupled with action which resulted in an increase of power.
Four months after Max returned from his mission, he and Anna
were married in the Bountiful Utah Temple.

Those same principles of faith were discovered by Amanda
Smith, a survivor of the Haun's Mill massacre. She was baptized
by Elder Orson Hyde in April 1831 when she was twenty-two
years old. She and her husband and family faced mob violence
and were forced to leave Kirtland, Ohio, in 1838. They went to
Missouri, taking only what they could carry in their wagon. The
following narrative is from *The Women of Mormondom,* by
Edward W. Tullidge, as written by Amanda Smith:

> We sold our beautiful home in Kirtland for a song, and trav-
> eled all summer to Missouri—our teams poor, and with hardly
> enough to keep body and soul together.
>
> We arrived in Caldwell county, near Haun's Mill, nine wag-
> ons of us in company. Two days before we arrived we were taken
> prisoners by an armed mob that had demanded every bit of
> ammunition and every weapon we had. We surrendered all.
> They knew it, for they searched our wagons.
>
> A few miles more brought us to Haun's Mill, where that
> awful scene of murder was enacted. My husband pitched his tent
> by a blacksmith's shop.
>
> Brother David Evans made a treaty with the mob that they
> would not molest us. He came just before the massacre and
> called the company together and they knelt in prayer.
>
> I sat in my tent. Looking up I suddenly saw the mob com-
> ing—the same that took away our weapons. They came like so
> many demons or wild Indians.
>
> Before I could get to the blacksmith's shop door to alarm
> the brethren, who were at prayers, the bullets were whistling
> amongst them. I seized my two little girls and escaped across the

mill-pond on a slab-walk. Another sister fled with me. Yet though we were women, with tender children, in flight for our lives, the demons poured volley after volley to kill us.

A number of bullets entered my clothes, but I was not wounded. . . .

When the firing had ceased I went back to the scene of the massacre, for there were my husband and three sons, of whose fate I as yet knew nothing. . . .

. . . Emerging from the blacksmith shop was my eldest son, bearing on his shoulders his little brother Alma.

"Oh! My Alma is dead!" I cried in anguish.

"No, mother; I think Alma is not dead. But father and brother Sardius are killed!"

What an answer was this to appal me! My husband and son murdered; another little son seemingly mortally wounded; and perhaps before the dreadful night should pass the murderers would return and complete their work!

But I could not weep then. The fountain of tears was dry; the heart overburdened with its calamity, and all the mother's sense absorbed in its anxiety for the precious boy which God alone could save by his miraculous aid.

The entire hip joint of my wounded boy had been shot away. Flesh, hip bone, joint and all had been ploughed out from the muzzle of the gun which the ruffian placed to the child's hip through the logs of the shop and deliberately fired.

We laid little Alma on a bed in our tent and I examined the wound. It was a ghastly sight. I knew not what to do. It was night now.

There were none left from that terrible scene, throughout that long, dark night, but about half a dozen bereaved and lamenting women, and the children. Eighteen or nineteen, all grown men excepting my murdered boy and another about the same age, were dead or dying; several more of the men were wounded, hiding away, whose groans through the night too well disclosed their hiding places, while the rest of the men had fled, at the moment of the massacre, to save their lives. The women were sobbing, in the greatest anguish of spirit; the children were

crying loudly with fear and grief at the loss of fathers and brothers; the dogs howled over their dead masters and the cattle were
terrified with the scent of the blood of the murdered.

Yet was I there, all that long, dreadful night, with my dead
and my wounded, and none but God as our physician and help.

Oh my Heavenly Father, I cried, what shall I do? Thou
seest my poor wounded boy and knowest my inexperience
(*The Women of Mormondom* [New York: n.p., 1877], pp.
121–24).

Let's look at the principles of faith as they relate to Sister
Smith. She joined the Church and followed the members
through difficult times. Many of those early members fell away
when the mobs threatened violence. She and her husband could
have denied their testimonies, but they remained firm, leaving
most of their worldly possessions, and followed the faithful from
Kirtland to Missouri. Their faithful actions didn't bring immediate rewards, but that night, in the worst of earthly situations,
Amanda Smith received the promised power.

Elder Mark E. Petersen put it this way: "Through all the tri-
als and tribulations of this world, if we will but pray . . .—'Jesus,
Savior, pilot me'—we shall go through life successfully, not free
from troubles and trials, but always accompanied by the Holy
Spirit, who will see us safely through" ("Blessings in Self-
Reliance," *Ensign*, May 1981, p. 61).

Amanda earnestly prayed, then listened and responded obe-
diently to the voice that gave her simple step-by-step directions
for dressing and treating that terrible wound. Although the entire
hip joint had been destroyed, little Alma eventually fully recov-
ered, a miracle bearing witness of the faith of his mother. Sister
Smith's story continues:

I cannot leave the tragic story without relating some inci-
dents of those five weeks when I was a prisoner with my
wounded boy in Missouri, near the scene of the massacre,
unable to obey the order of extermination.

All the Mormons in the neighborhood had fled out of the

State, excepting a few families of the bereaved women and children who had gathered at the house of Brother David Evans, two miles from the scene of the massacre. To this house Alma had been carried after that fatal night.

In our utter desolation, what could we women do but pray? Prayer was our only source of comfort; our Heavenly Father our only helper. None but he could save and deliver us.

One day a mobber came from the mill with the captain's fiat: "The captain says if you women don't stop your d——d prayer he will send down a posse and kill every d——d one of you!"

And he might as well have done it, as to stop us poor women praying in that hour of our great calamity.

Our prayers were hushed in terror. We dared not let our voices be heard in the house in supplication. I could pray in my bed or in silence, but I could not live thus long. This godless silence was more intolerable than had been that night of the massacre.

I could bear it no longer. I pined to hear once more my own voice in petition to my Heavenly Father.

I stole down into a corn-field, and crawled into a "stout of corn." It was as the temple of the Lord to me at that moment. I prayed aloud and most fervently. When I emerged from the corn a voice spoke to me. It was a voice as plain as I ever heard one. It was no silent, strong impression of the spirit, but a *voice*, repeating a verse of the saint's hymn:

> That soul who on Jesus hath leaned for repose,
> I cannot, I will not, desert to its foes;
> That soul, though all hell should endeavor to shake,
> I'll never, no never, no never forsake!

From that moment I had no more fear. I felt that nothing could hurt me (ibid., pp. 129–30).

Fear was replaced by faithful action, which brought increased faith devoid of fear. Now Sister Smith had a power that no demon in this world or another could match:

Soon after this the mob sent us word that unless we were all out of the State by a certain day we should be killed.

The day came, and at evening came fifty armed men to execute the sentence.

I met them at the door. They demanded of me why I was not gone? I bade them enter and see their own work. They crowded into my room and I showed them my wounded boy. They came, party after party, until all had seen my excuse. Then they quarreled among themselves and came near fighting.

At last they went away, all but two. These I thought were detailed to kill us. Then the two returned.

"Madam," said one, "have you any meat in the house?"

"No," was my reply.

"Could you dress a fat hog if one was laid at your door?"

"I think we could!" was my answer.

And then they went and caught a fat hog from a herd which had belonged to a now exiled brother, killed it and dragged it to my door, and departed.

These men, who had come to murder us, left on the threshold of our door a meat offering to atone for their repented intention.

Yet even when my son was well I could not leave the State, now accursed indeed to the saints.

The mob had taken my horses, as they had the drove of horses, and the beeves, and the hogs, and wagons, and the tents, of the murdered and exiled.

So I went down into Davies county (ten miles) to Captain Comstock, and demanded of him my horses. There was one of them in his yard. He said I could have it if I paid five dollars for its keep. I told him I had no money.

I did not fear the captain of the mob, for I had the Lord's promise that nothing should hurt me. But his wife swore that the mobbers were fools for not killing the women and children as well as the men—declaring that we would "breed up a pack ten times worse than the first."

I left without the captain's permission to take my horse, or giving pay for its keep; but I went into his yard and took it, and returned to our refuge unmolested.

Learning that my other horse was at the mill, I next yoked up a pair of steers to a sled and went and demanded it also (ibid., pp.130–31).

Faith coupled with action led to power. Sister Smith's faith didn't prevent trials, but gave her strength to endure. No life is without trials, and for good reason. Elder Richard G. Scott said:

> To exercise faith is to trust that the Lord knows what He is doing with you and that He can accomplish it for your eternal good even though you cannot understand how He can possibly do it. We are like infants in our understanding of eternal matters and their impact on us here in mortality. Yet at times we act as if we knew it all. When you pass through trials for His purposes, as you trust Him, exercise faith in Him, He will help you. That support will generally come step by step, a portion at a time. While you are passing through each phase, the pain and diffi- culty that comes from being enlarged will continue. If all mat- ters were immediately resolved at your first petition, you could not grow. Your Father in Heaven and His Beloved Son love you perfectly. They would not require you to experience a moment more of difficulty than is absolutely needed for your personal benefit or for that of those you love ("Trust in the Lord," *Ensign*, Nov. 1995, p. 17).

Those moments of difficulty sometimes seem eternal. Trust- ing our Heavenly Father and his Son also means trusting their timetable for our desired blessings. On this subject, there is no lack of comforting material. We as Latter-day Saint sisters have easy access to the words of prophets, both past and present, that we know represent words of comfort, hope, and peace from our Heavenly Father. That faith and confidence in our prophets can replace many fears. Study their words. When coupled with your faith in the calling of a prophet, their words are filled with peace. Are you a single sister? Listen to a prophet: "Not all women in the Church will have an opportunity for marriage and mother-hood in mortality. But if you in this situation are worthy and endure faithfully, you can be assured of all blessings from a kind and loving Heavenly Father—and I emphasize *all* blessings" (*The Teachings of Ezra Taft Benson* [Salt Lake City: Bookcraft, 1988], p. 550).

Are you married but struggling with infertility? Listen to a prophet:

> Many of the sisters grieve because they are not blessed with off-spring. You will see the time when you will have millions of children around you. If you are faithful to your covenants, you will be mothers of nations. . . . And when you have assisted in peopling one earth, there are millions of earths still in the course of creation. And when they have endured a thousand million times longer than this earth, it is only as it were the beginning of your creations. Be faithful, and if you are not blest with children in this time, you will be hereafter" (Brigham Young, *Journal of Discourses* 8:208).

Are you a mother of a prodigal son or daughter? Elder Jeffrey R. Holland spoke at the Tooele Utah North Stake conference and asked the congregation if any were worried about their children. He asked if they would like something that would guarantee the continuance of the entire family throughout eternity. My ears and heart were riveted on his answer. Straying children had captured extensive prayer and fear had engulfed much of my personal time. Elder Holland continued, "Then keep the covenants you have made in the temple." He raised his hands, clasped them together, and brought them down on the podium to emphasize the promise that the seal of those covenants cannot be broken by any power—not even Satan himself.

I had recently read Orson F. Whitney's statement:

> The Prophet Joseph Smith declared—and he never taught more comforting doctrine—that the eternal sealings of faithful

parents and the divine promises made to them for valiant service in the Cause of Truth, would save not only themselves, but likewise their posterity. Though some of the sheep may wander, the eye of the Shepherd is upon them, and sooner or later they will feel the tentacles of Divine Providence reaching out after them and drawing them back to the fold. Either in this life or in the life to come, they will return. They will have to pay their debt to justice; they will suffer for their sins; and may tread a thorny path; but if it leads them at last, like the penitent Prodigal, to a loving and forgiving father's heart and home, the painful experience will not have been in vain. Pray for your careless and disobedient children; hold on to them with your faith. Hope on, trust on, till you see the salvation of God (in Conference Report, Apr. 1929, p. 110).

His comforting message was restated in our day by Elder Boyd K. Packer: "We cannot overemphasize the value of temple marriage, the binding ties of the sealing ordinance, and the standards of worthiness required of them. When parents keep the covenants they have made at the altar of the temple, their children will be forever bound to them" ("Our Moral Environment," *Ensign*, May 1992, p. 68).

The fear that had engulfed me lifted and was replaced by my faith in the prophets of the Lord. Later, after updating and printing my pedigree chart, I noticed that my Grandfather Fernelius had the letters BEPSC next to his name. The letters stood for completed ordinances. Grandpa had been **B**aptized, **E**ndowed, sealed to his **P**arents, sealed to his **S**pouse, and his **C**hildren's ordinances were all complete. The C missing next to my name prompted me to write these lines while basking in the quiet peace of my new understanding:

B. E. P. S. & C.

A small, quiet seed lay dormant in me.
The time was not right. Could it be

That someday my life would leave me some time
To find the parts of my family tree?

Grandparents alive to ask questions firsthand
Would have made my search breeze along.
No, I'd wait 'til they'd gone to the other side;
Then who'd know where the names would belong?

Soon came high school and college . . . wasn't that fun?
Then Max Molgard entered my life.
Across the altar we joined hands as one
Becoming eternal husband and wife.

The children came quickly and filled up my days
With diapers, then car pools, then worries.
Was I doing it right? I was trying my best,
Though the years went by in a flurry.

As the children began to go on their own
Some on the path, some chose to stray,
My small little seed was beginning to grow
'Til Elijah declared, "It's your day!"

Working the puzzle of my family tree,
The fathers, the children, the mothers;
And feeling the joy of binding them fast . . .
Spiritual hugs; highs like no others.

I printed my pedigree chart last week,
And smiled as I patted my back.
The bold letters in caps stood out and declared
Covenants made; blanks meant a lack.

B stands for Baptized, E means Endowed
PS, sealed to Parents and Spouse.
But the golden letter that's hardest to get
Links hands all over the house.

What kind of a house you ask, and I'll say
Israel's House is the name of our tree.
And when the children's ordinances are done,

We complete with a capital C.

All the work that I've done . . . and there's still a hole,
Though C's are all over my tree.
The one that I long for and want most of all
Is the one by the name that is me.

What would I give for that C on my chart?
My Father in Heaven knows me.
I've told him He can have all that I have,
Just bless me with capital C.

"All my life I will labor thy kingdom to build,
Take my time, hear my prayers as I plead.
My husband is thine, all the hours thou wants,
Our hands are thine to meet others' needs."

When I look at the distance some children must turn
My tears wet my pillow at the girth.
Then the quiet peace comes from the Spirit and
Those that speak for our Father on earth.

"Are you keeping the promises made in my house?
Are your covenants still firm and strong?
No power on earth can break that strong seal.
Be patient, I'll bring them along.

"They're part of my House of Israel, you know.
They've made choices that brought them to you.
Elijah, who turned you to your ancestor's work
Will turn the hearts of your children too.

"And one of these days in a temple of mine
As you wait in a room past the veil,
Not only Max and Michelle will come through
But McKay and Barbie as well.

"Then patiently wait and love them along
Please, love unconditionally.
And Leslie will come, yes Kenny too.
No empty chairs . . . B. E. P. S. & C."

As President Gordon B. Hinckley so confidently said: "We have nothing to fear. God is at the helm. He will overrule for the good of this work. He will shower down blessings upon those who walk in obedience to His commandments. Such has been His promise. Of His ability to keep that promise none of us can doubt" ("This Is the Work of the Master," *Ensign,* May 1995, p. 69).

Timely
Priorities

SUSA YOUNG GATES ONCE asked her father, President Brigham Young, "how it would ever be possible to accomplish the great amount of temple work that must be done, if all are given a full opportunity for exaltation. He told her there would be many inventions of labor-saving devices, so that our daily duties could be performed in a short time" (Archibald F. Bennett, "Put On Thy Strength, O Zion!" *Improvement Era*, Oct. 1952, p. 720).

Prior to Brigham Young's prophetic statement, horses had been the main means of transportation with no significant changes for six thousand years. Laborsaving devices had been few and far between. The restoration of the gospel brought with it a responsibility to spread the word to the four corners of the earth. Early missionaries trudged by foot, and took lengthy boat passages.

Then the telegraph ushered in a burst of inventions that sent Brigham Young's prophetic statement ringing through the corridors of time to our day. Computers have enhanced scripture study, sped genealogical research, and compacted and organized records. Planes and automobiles whisk us to destinations near and far. General conference is seen worldwide through satellite and television.

Inventions in the home have given women the gift of freedom from spending the day in food preparations and laundry. I can sit at the computer and type while simultaneously making bread, doing laundry, and doing my dishes. What a day to be alive! These inventions didn't just happen by chance during our day. Joseph Fielding Smith spoke during the 1926 general conference and his words are even more applicable today:

> I maintain that had there been no restoration of the gospel, and no organization of the Church of Jesus Christ of Latter-day Saints, there would have been no radio; there would have been no airplane, and there would not have been . . . other things wherein the world has been benefitted by such discoveries. Under such conditions these blessings would have been withheld, for they belong to the Dispensation of the Fulness of Times of which the restoration of the gospel and the organization of the Church constitute the central point, from which radiates the Spirit of the Lord throughout the world. The inspiration of the Lord has gone out and takes hold of the minds of men, though they know it not, and they are directed by the Lord. In this manner he brings them into his service that his purposes and his righteousness, in due time, may be supreme on the earth.
>
> . . . I do not believe for one moment that these discoveries have come by chance, or that they have come because of superior intelligence possessed by men today over those who lived in ages that are past. They have come and are coming because the time is ripe, because the Lord has willed it, and because he had poured out his Spirit on all flesh (in Conference Report, Oct. 1926, p. 117).

The result, as prophesied, has been an abundance of discretionary time. Free of much of the often mundane, but vital for survival tasks, we have choices our pioneer ancestors only dreamed about. Those choices have left us wide open to wonderful experiences and, conversely, to Satan's careful plans. Can you imagine his panic as he saw what we could do with our "extra" time? He cannot leave covenant daughters of God alone to fill their lives with positive steps back to our Maker. He does not want us to fill the measure of our creation. Consequently, he has devised several schemes that mess up the effectiveness of our choices.

His first method of attack (plan A) is to entice us to make wrong choices. Given the choice between good and evil, with the gift of the Holy Ghost, we often are able to make right choices. When that method is ineffective, Satan uses priority plan B and priority plan C.

Plan B involves wearing ourselves out in good service. Who do you think came up with the idea of "running faster than we have strength"? (see D&C 10:4). Also, this plan introduces inappropriate guilt. Remember, "false guilt, inappropriate guilt, can be just as destructive as if it were ordinary sin. The Spirit of the Lord never teaches excessive guilt, but Satan does" (Errol R. Fish, *Promptings of the Spirit* [Mesa, AZ: Cogent Publishing, 1990], p. 144). Overcoming Satan's priority plan B involves understanding the order of priorities and eliminating guilt when we know we have made a good decision (even if it eliminates another good decision). Anne Osborn Poelman explains:

> While there are surely some major decisions that must be made between right and morally wrong choices, for most of us the greater difficulty comes in choosing between two equally correct alternatives. Most choices we face are therefore not between right and wrong but between right and right. Few of us have to choose between holding family home evening and robbing a bank. More often the most difficult decisions are between equally attractive, worthy activities. Should we can the fruit that is now perfectly ripe or go on a much-needed date with our partner? Should we get in the long overdue temple session or take the children on an outing? ("Balance: The Joy of Perspective," *LDS Women's Treasury* [Salt Lake City: Deseret Book Co., 1997], pp. 112–13).

Does this territory have a familiar ring? In a devotional at Brigham Young University, Bruce C. Hafen, then president of Ricks College, related the suppressed frustration of an overworked, somewhat harassed young mother who, when advised to "just be sure you put the Lord's work first," blurted out in near desperation, "But what if it is all the Lord's work?" (See "On Dealing with Uncertainty," *Ensign*, Aug. 1979, p. 64).

A concerned physician similarly frustrated with time constraints asked President Harold B. Lee for guidance. The prophetic answer works equally as well for women as for men: The first responsibility is to self, then to family, then to the Church (see *The Teachings of Harold B. Lee*, ed. Clyde J. Williams [Salt Lake City: Bookcraft, 1996], p. 614).

Sister Patricia Holland reinforced this vision of prioritizing responsibilities when she asked:

> How can we be fully successful wives or mothers or missionaries or temple workers or citizens or neighbors if we are not trying to bring our best self to these tasks? . . .
>
> My oldest child tried to teach me this principle years ago. I had not been feeling well on a day I had promised to take this then three-year-old son to the zoo. As my aches and pains increased, I finally said in exasperation, "Matthew, I don't know if we should go to the zoo and take care of you or if we should stay home and take care of mother." He looked up at me for a moment with his big brown eyes and then stated emphatically, "Mama, I think *you* should take care of *you*, so *you* can take care of *me*." He was wise enough even at that age to know where his best interests were ultimately served. Unless we take care of ourselves, it's virtually impossible to properly take care of others ("Portraits of Eve: God's Promises of Personal Identity," *LDS Women's Treasury*, pp. 95–96).

Taking care of ourselves includes listening to warning signals that sound whenever we are pushing our physical or spiritual limits. There is a similar mechanism in an airplane called a stall warning device. The sensors measure the air flow out on the wings and sound a warning series of high beeps when the plane is getting close to stalling. The closer you get to a nosedive, the more shrill the sound.

We all have days when a sick child, a deadline, or some other circumstance has started our stall warning device beeping. As soon as possible, listen and respond to the warning. That is the point that you become your own best physician by putting your needs on the top of the priority list. You ask, "Isn't that selfish?" That comment shows you how effective Satan is. If you take a nosedive, how many things are you going to be able to do for others? What will be the cost in time, money, and emotional recovery? If your stall warning device is constantly beeping, a change is critical. You know, or experience will soon teach you, what your physical and emotional limits are. Your limits will not mirror your neighbor's or your sister's. They are yours. Listen to what your body is telling you. Does it need more exercise? Make arrangements. Does it need more sleep? Make it a priority. Do you need help because you can't see a way to make changes? Work within your circle of family, friends, and Church leaders. Surely they have needs you can meet in exchange for helping you meet yours.

Failure to establish proper priorities will leave us like Martha in the New Testament. Picture having Jesus as your guest. Martha, along with her sister Mary, sat at his feet to learn eternal truths. Mary sat back and enjoyed the spiritual nourishment, but Martha was a worrier. I can feel her anxiety as she stewed: "It's almost time for dinner, and I wasn't expecting such an important guest. What will he think if I prepare a less-than-perfect meal? Oh, what am I going to fix?" She eventually jumped up to prepare a meal, but felt overwhelmed with the task at hand and asked Jesus to ask Mary to help her.

Luke writes that "Martha was cumbered about much serving" (Luke 10:40); and Jesus tenderly reproved her by saying, "Martha, Martha, thou art careful and troubled about many things" (v. 41). Looking at the bottom of the page, the footnote tells us that *careful* means *worried*. Elder Neal A. Maxwell explains: "The conversation that night was eternal; the calories were not. When we get filled with Martha-like anxiety, it usually stems from failure to establish proper priorities" (*Deposition of a Disciple* [Salt Lake City: Deseret Book Co., 1976], p. 69).

Evelyn T. Marshall wrote a beautiful article about Mary and Martha. She writes:

> In a sense, Jesus is teaching a concept that could well be applied to many situations that require us to judge how to use a limited amount of time and energy. It is quite possible, for example, for a teacher to spend more time and effort on the table centerpiece and posters than on preparing the meat of a lesson. But is that choosing "the good part"? . . .
>
> . . . When deciding which part should receive emphasis . . . sisters would do well to seek the Spirit as a guide.
>
> "If the decision is right, they will feel at peace. That is the key. If they have made the wrong decisions, they will tend to feel troubled." (Barbara Winder, *Ensign*, Mar. 1986, p. 21.) *Troubled* is, in fact, the very word that Jesus uses to describe Martha on that occasion when she may have been confused regarding her own priorities. (See Luke 10:41.) ("Mary and Martha—Faithful Sisters, Devoted Disciples," *Ensign*, Jan. 1987, pp. 30–31).

That is the principle for making priority-based decisions. Are you troubled? If you are troubled about something that encourages you to make productive changes, listen and obey. It is the Spirit's prompting that will help you to use your time productively. When you have done all in your power and still feel troubled, you need to seek help from family, friends, and Church leaders. Prayers are often answered through our mortal circle of acquaintances and through reading the scriptures. Sitting in a meeting of any kind we can be edified (taught what we need to know) by the Spirit. The Holy Ghost is a powerful teacher and will give you individual instruction. I often smile when someone thanks me specifically for what they learned in the Gospel Doctrine class, reminding them that their understanding was gleaned from what the Spirit was teaching that day. The Spirit had covered something I hadn't consciously taught. With the help of all of these sources, you should eventually be able to put your life in the proper order and find peace.

Let me cushion that statement with a warning: that peaceful feeling can be masked by Satan's counterfeit of inappropriate guilt. False guilt does not lead to productive results or changes. It comes barging in to cancel happiness and peace even when a good decision has been made. It whispers, for example, "I know that your son needs you at his program, but Sister Nash has worked so hard at putting together this special homemaking night. Didn't you raise your hand to sustain her as Relief Society president? How can you sit and enjoy his program when you aren't attending homemaking night?"

When you have done all that is in your power, drop the guilt and enjoy the benefits of a good choice (even though it may eliminate another good choice).

Anne Osborn Poelman identified Satan's priority plan C when she said: "Let us remember that one of the great learning experiences of this life is not only to make the right decisions, but also to sequence them properly. The configuration or priority of correct choices is as important as the choices themselves. To choose not only wisely but also timely and well brings to us the joy of a balanced, productive life" ("Balance: The Joy of Perspective," *LDS Women's Treasury,* p. 112).

The importance of timing is illustrated in this story from long ago: A young girl named Nika listened to the missionaries in a faraway land. Although she was tender in years, her testimony burned brightly and within weeks her desire to join the Saints in Zion was so strong that she decided to leave her land and family and immigrate to America. Before boarding the great boat that would take her far away, she listened to the advice from her elders and carefully took notes, promising to precisely follow every direction. "Nika," they advised, "life in America is full of blessings and promises that can be yours if you work hard and prepare for each season. As soon as you arrive, plant seeds to prepare for the next season when you will weed and harvest your crops. Spend the following season preparing your foods for storage. Then, because of your preparations, you will enjoy a season of resting and pampering yourself with activities you have been too busy to enjoy previously."

Nika's ocean voyage was long and arduous. A severe storm blew the ship off course and necessitated spending extra weeks at sea. Once in America, extreme weather also delayed her departure to the West. By the time she arrived in the valley of the Great Salt Lake, the leaves were alive with the brilliant colors of the fall.

Unaccustomed to the seasons of the West, Nika set about to follow the important instructions. Though there was a nip in the air she carefully placed her seeds in a shallow trough she had carved across the hardened earth and waited expectantly for the following season, anticipating her tender care and eventually an abundant harvest.

We can all picture Nika's distress and discouragement as she tried to dig in the snow seeking weeds and harvest. Poor Nika thought she was following instructions. In her defense, she was following specific directions and her actions were not wrong. She was doing right things in the wrong seasons.

Very early in the history of the Latter-day Saints, Satan introduced plan C, which consisted of talking the Saints into doing right things in the wrong season, and the Lord had to take corrective measure. Only four months had elapsed since the Church was organized and Joseph Smith had more than his fair share of problems. Persecution was intense, he had a young family to support, and he and Oliver Cowdery were told, "Thou wast called and chosen to write the Book of Mormon, and to my ministry" (D&C 24:1).

Picture the stress on Joseph Smith. A man of any worth takes care of his family, which in those days was a full-time occupation. That had to be a right thing. He needed to keep them safe. That had to be a right thing. He needed to lead and instruct the Church. That was a right thing. The Bible needed to be translated correctly. How was he ever going to get it all done? The

Lord explained about doing right things in the right season:

> I have lifted thee up out of thine afflictions, and have counseled thee, that thou hast been delivered from all thine enemies, and thou hast been delivered from the powers of Satan and from darkness! . . .
>
> Magnify thine office; and after thou hast sowed thy fields and secured them, go speedily unto the church which is in Colesville, Fayette, and Manchester, and they shall support thee. . . .
>
> For thou shalt devote all thy service in Zion; and in this thou shalt have strength. . . .
>
> And in temporal labors thou shalt not have strength, for this is not thy calling (D&C 24:1, 3, 7, 9).

They were doing their best, so the Lord was protecting them; the Church members were to take care of their temporal worries; and they were to work full-time at their service in Zion. They would not have strength, even in doing right things, if it was not their calling. Every season of our lives presents a parallel and a fine opportunity for Satan to talk us into doing right things out of that season.

Let's look at some parallels in a woman's world. It will eventually be right to feed a baby solid foods, but feeding SpaghettiOs to a newborn daughter would be disastrous. That baby will someday be able to walk, but standing her up at six months and letting go could be dangerous. When she becomes a Beehive and goes to camp, a wise camp leader will not expect her and her fellow teenagers to be oozing with charity. If she does, she will find herself frustrated with their inability to unconditionally give to others while still in their tutoring season.

What season do you find yourself in? Are you single and free to decide between serving a mission, soaking in knowledge at school, or using your talents to enjoy an exciting career? You may be the same age as someone who is married. Just like a menu at a restaurant, when you choose a hamburger, you won't get the chicken. The sister that marries makes a choice to move into another season. The mission choice is off the menu. A full-time mission is a wonderful choice in its season, but not for a newly-married sister. Our newly-married sister can continue to go to school and have a full-time job until she moves into the next season: motherhood. Again, she will need to prayerfully reassess her priorities. She can take much comfort in knowing the Lord "shall gently lead those that are with young" (Isaiah 40:11).

Reaching decisions, even as they relate to Church activity, needs to take into consideration divine callings such as wife and mother. President Ezra Taft Benson said it best: "When we put God first, all other things fall into their proper place or drop out of our lives. Our love of the Lord must govern the claims for our affection, the demands on our time, the interests we pursue, and the order of our priorities ("The Great Commandment—Love the Lord," *Ensign*, May 1988, p. 4).

Remember, as Elder Marion G. Romney said: "Of this we may be sure: to make the proper choice on any issue is of far more importance to us personally than is the immediate outcome of the issue upon which we make a decision. The choices we make will affect the scope of our agency in the future. As of now, we have the right of decision. What we will have tomorrow will depend upon how we decide today" (from Marion G. Romney Funeral Address, 23 May 1988, quoted by Lucile C. Tate in *Boyd K. Packer: A Watchman on the Tower* [Salt Lake City: Bookcraft, 1995], p. 240).

Care for our eternal callings as mothers, daughters, and wives is only a piece of the puzzle of priorities, and Satan will incite confusion. Remember what is at stake. Your little ones "cannot sin, for power is not given unto Satan to tempt little children, until they begin to become accountable before me" (D&C 29:47). During those foundational eight years children need to be taught (like the two thousand stripling warriors) by their mothers. No one else, except the father, has been given the divine power of discernment and unconditional love for that child. If Satan can divert a mother's attention away from her child, he has won a most important battle. Unfortunately, the menu of possibilities doesn't change considerably with life's changing seasons. The only change is the increasing volume of voices advertising menu items and degrading correct individual choices. Sister Ardeth G. Kapp explains:

> Even as we endeavor to play our various parts in their appropriate seasons, there will continually be self-appointed stage managers who, not knowing or caring about the script, will shout from the wings, "You're playing the wrong part. You don't want the supporting role. That isn't important. Why be a supporting actor when you can be the star? Be front stage. Move in. Let them know who you are. This is your chance to win the applause."
>
> There are those who would attempt to revise, rewrite, and restructure the script, changing the sacred roles of men and women, modifying the scenes and seasons, adjusting the morals and models where possible, and even altering the main stage, the home, in which the most important drama of life should unfold.
>
> There are always loud voices assuming authorship while abdicating stewardship. You and I may never win acclaim, and society may never know us beyond the street where we live, or because one calling or position may be in the public eye more than another. But I am sure that when the lights have gone out and the curtain is closed on our second act, the opinions of others, the acceptance and applause of the crowd, will be a haunting echo if our Father's approval is in question" (*My Neighbor, My Sister, My Friend* [Salt Lake City: Deseret Book Co., 1990], p. 7).

A loud and pleading word of caution needs to be said. Judgment is so easy for those not living another's life. What is right for you might not be right for someone else, even if they appear to be in the same circumstances. We were taught this concept when we moved from Utah to Florida. The members there looked the same as we did. They acted the same as we did. They didn't talk the same, but we loved the lilt of their Southern accents. When it came time to plant a garden, we never questioned exactly how to do it. We thought we had already learned how to in Utah. We would prepare the soil, smooth it out, plant the seeds at the proper depth, and hoe ditches to allow for watering.

Our friends chuckled at our methods. Although they looked the same, they were living in different circumstances, and had made proper adjustments. The gardens in Florida looked like someone had been playing in the sandpile. Rows of foot-high mounds kept the water from molding the newly-planted seeds. An irrigation ditch didn't make much sense in a place that received daily downpours of rain. Visit with the Lord about the best thing for you in your circumstances, recognizing your answer may not be a universal one.

Answers may also vary for those who find themselves in the difficult situation of needing to leave home to earn money because of death, divorce, or other extenuating circumstances. They can only prayerfully counsel with the Lord to put in place the very best situation under difficult circumstances and then diligently block Satan's inappropriate guilt from overwhelming their precious family time.

Try to enjoy each season. Find satisfaction in every part of your life without wishing it away. Each season has growth-inspiring hazards and glorious possibilities. Kathleen Bushnell Jensen gives us wonderful advice:

> When I had several small children, I tended to look at women who were out doing things—taking institute classes, tole painting, skiing—and I would think, "How do they do it? I'm so unorganized." As I look back, my advice is to be content where you are. If you have young children, enjoy them! I'm old enough to know that you don't have young children very long. Those moments are fleeting. Don't wish away your toddlers and bright-eyed preschoolers. They will never be yours at that age again. Don't rush your seasons. I feel the most off balance when I'm trying to run faster than I have strength, when I'm trying to keep up with people who are single or who maybe don't have as many children at home. Our needs are different. When you

have small children, you don't need to have a totally spotless home. When I go into a home that is full of young children and yet is totally spotless, I think, "What do the kids do all day? Live outdoors?" Be realistic; let your kids have some fun. Let them make messes. Don't worry about what everyone might be thinking. And don't compare your home to anyone else's (*Women and Christ: Living the Abundant Life,* ed. Dawn Hall Anderson, Susette Fletcher Green, and Marie Cornwall [Salt Lake City: Deseret Book Co., 1993], pp. 51–52).

Seasons of motherhood mingle together with a variety of children's ages, but the next significant season is when all of the children are in school. There is a window of opportunity, during school hours, when menu choices previously abstained from may become right choices in right seasons. Classes might be taken and careers begun, with a few words of caution. What starts as a few hours after the children are in school and before they come home often spreads out to engulf more hours until it becomes a major focus. Latter-day Saint women know what they value most and when what they value most doesn't get the most attention because of choices they have made, they feel frustrated and troubled.

Even when children are in school, there are critical parenting times. President Ezra Taft Benson taught about the important crossroads when he said:

> Mothers in Zion, your God-given roles are so vital to your own exaltation and to the salvation and exaltation of your family. A child needs a mother more than all the things money can buy. Spending time with your children is the greatest gift of all. . . .
>
> . . .Take time to always be at the crossroads when your children are either coming or going—when they leave and return from dates—when they bring friends home. Be there at the crossroads whether your children are six or sixteen (*The Teachings of Ezra Taft Benson* [Salt Lake City: Bookcraft, 1988], pp. 515–16).

Every phase of a child's life presents a new challenge for Satan and he responds with customized attacks. A child left to himself doesn't have much of a chance. When they are fifteen, they have had seven years of Satan-stopping experience and he has had six thousand years of experience tempting teenagers. His approach with them matches their changing mortal bodies.

When McKay was about ten years old, he was fascinated by the Olympics. Every second he could watch the competition, he sat riveted to the television. One day I sat down to watch the ceremony at which medals were being handed out. McKay watched intently, then turned and asked, "Mom, would you be proud of me if I got ten gold medals?" Sensing a teaching moment, I replied, "Yes, I would be proud of you if you earned ten medals. But there are some things that you can do that would bring me more pride than Olympic glory ever would. Watching you serve a worthy mission and then come home and get married in the temple would be the best way you could make me pop my buttons."

He considered my answer then responded, "I'm going to go on a mission, but I don't think I'll get married in the temple." My heart dropped. After years of careful instruction, my son had already decided against a temple marriage. I carefully inquired, "Why won't you be getting married in the temple?" He looked at me, wrinkled his nose, and explained, "I can't think of any girl I know that I'd want to spend eternity with." I knew we still had some time before worrying over the boy/girl problem with him.

Several years later I had just swallowed my last bite of dinner and Max had just filled his mouth when McKay asked, "Dad, what are hormones?" Seeing that I was in the position of being able to answer immediately Max pointed at his mouth and then pointed at me. Everyone looked expectantly in my direction and Max chose to not chew until I had begun my explanation, just in case the conversation might boomerang back to him. I began: "Hormones are little things that are asleep inside your body. In a couple of years, they will wake up and when that happens, you will start to like girls." McKay seemed totally satisfied with that answer and concluded, "I hope mine just stay asleep." With that, he put on his baseball hat and left to play catch with a friend. We were still safe. But Satan sometimes is aware of our child's shift before we are. Sadly, we lose our greatest battles to him when our children are between the ages of sixteen and twenty-five. There are so many life-changing choices for them to make, but they spend so much time outside the home at that age that it is easy for us to think we have moved into a new season, and are finished with our intensive parenting.

Last year, McKay turned fifteen about the time that I decided my season had shifted. He was our only child at home and has always been very independent. I was job sharing a second grade classroom and worked every morning from eight o'clock until noon after dropping McKay off at the high school. It was the perfect job, but my love and longings had always been in the medical field. Before I had married, I had taken the prerequisites for a career in that field, applied for acceptance, and, notwithstanding my high G. P. A., had not been accepted because I was engaged. (This was, of course, twenty-six years ago.) I transferred my credits to the university Max was attending. There was no choice in the medical field, but I was told I could have a science concentration filled and lose no credits if I transferred to elementary education. I reluctantly finished and after my children were in school, had been surprised at how much I enjoyed teaching.

Observing the miracle of birth as my granddaughter was born rekindled my interest in medicine. I love the delivery room and decided the time was right for me to pursue a nursing degree. After checking around, I found that the college Max commutes to every day to teach institute had a nursing program. They would accept all of the science classes I had already taken if I would just take pathophysiology to review anatomy and physiology. My long-ago excitement got percolating. I quit my teaching job and enrolled for fall quarter. The pathophysiology, chemistry, and nutrition classes that quarter would complete my prerequisites for the nursing program. The schedule necessitated five-days-a-week attendance, and it only made sense for me to go with

Max. I added an institute class and instead of walking every day with my friend at home, I made new friends and started walking at 7:00 A.M. with my associates at the college. I showered and dressed at the physical education facility after walking and was ready for my 9:00 A.M. class. We would return home about five o'clock in the afternoon.

We had a long talk with McKay. He seemed to be the only one besides me who was affected by my new schedule, and he didn't seem to mind getting himself up and off to school; in fact, he encouraged it. Football practice usually prevented him from coming home to an empty house.

The opportunity to find out my brain still functioned above a second grade level was stimulating, and for the first time in a long time, I was spending a lot of hours with my husband. I relished our togetherness.

Despite the positive list, I became troubled shortly after the quarter started. McKay's attendance, grades, and attitude all took a turn for the worse. Our older children were patient but a bit disappointed that I had disappeared from their lives. I was not only unavailable during the school hours, but homework kept me occupied at night. I didn't have time to do family history, play with the grandchildren, or study effectively to teach my Gospel Doctrine class on Sunday.

The quarter was soon over, and during the long Christmas break I was accepted into the nursing program. It was time to take another look at my options. The full menu was available, but choosing to be a nurse eliminated so many highly valued parts of my life. Sister Janath R. Cannon informs us that "Richard L. Evans once remarked that some things were *only* worth doing if they didn't have to be done so well that they interfered with more important things" ("Priorities in the Pursuit of Excellence," *Ensign*, Apr. 1976, p. 70). I spent several days and eventually one sleepless night pondering my priorities. My prayerful decision opened a spot in the nursing program.

I began to look for other possible ways to fill my wants without eliminating other needs. Our local hospital was looking for technicians to work in labor and delivery. They explained that the job, should I decide to accept it, would entail being on call for a twelve hour shift one day a week. I would more or less be a gopher for the doctor and nurses. There wouldn't be much money involved, but I would be in the delivery room and I wouldn't need any more schooling except specific training at the hospital. That choice made everything else fall into place as I filled the rest of the days of the week with all of the people and activities that were important to me.

My experience highlights how priorities work. We need to decide what is of most value, and arrange our schedules around that. Many of us have heard how priorities are like a bottle filled with rocks and sand. The rocks are those things of most value to you. You need to put them into the bottle first and then the sand fits nicely around them. If you fill the bottle with sand first, the rocks will overflow the bottle, leaving some important things out of your life.

When something happens and you notice that some important rocks are out of your life, you make adjustments. Day by day some important rocks may get placed aside, but overall the things of greatest value will be getting most of our attention.

President James E. Faust gave valuable advice that will help us all to choose our priorities: "Great women respond generously to their instincts to do good. With your very being held still, listen to the whisperings of the Holy Spirit. Follow those noble, intuitive feelings planted deep within your soul by Deity" ("A Message to My Granddaughters: Becoming 'Great Women'," *Ensign*, Sept. 1986, p. 20).

Those whisperings "will show unto you all things what ye should do" (2 Nephi 32:5). They will help you choose your priorities. Those whisperings will tell you if one good choice is better than the other. They will encourage guilt when productive choices need to be made and will also serve to eliminate inappropriate guilt. Those whisperings will tell you proper choices to make during each season of your life. Listen and respond, and feel the peace of living as your Father in Heaven wants you to live.

&

"Be Ye Therefore Perfect"

*H*ER NAME IS PATTY PERFECT and she looms, rivaled by no one, as an archenemy to Latter-day Saint women. She has a dozen children (all with perfect manners, always immaculately groomed, and dressed in handmade suits and dresses). No one ever raises their voice in her home. She has a full two-year supply of food, which she has bottled herself from her own garden and orchard. (Of course she couldn't get any of this done without those ever-willing children.) They have a wonderful system that gets the children up singing the hymns of Zion and gathering immediately for family prayer and scripture study before they make their beds, clean their rooms, pack their own lunches, and head for school (where they are all the top students of their classes). They spend Friday and Saturday evenings (but never Mondays, which are reserved for fabulous family home evenings) providing chamber music for wedding receptions, playing instruments that they rotate between themselves (because of their multiple instrument proficiencies), playing music they arranged while mingling around the table after supper one evening.

Alas, you find yourself in your typical home stacked high with laundry and littered with bookbags, shoes, and other various sundry items. If you have family scripture study, it's under protest. When you try to convince your son that a shower after football practice really is required, he puts on his hat, calling, "No time, Mom" and is gone. You're too weary to hassle him about the fact that he has just skipped practicing the piano for the third day in a row. Besides, the baby is screaming and your macaroni and cheese is burning.

It's difficult trying to appear as Mrs. Perfect to the outside world. Our daughter Barbie seemed to come into this world with specific instructions: "Your mission is to blow your mother's cover so the world will recognize her imperfections."

Let me humbly share one particularly memorable event: One Saturday morning I said good-bye to Max and decided the children and I would spend the day finding every item in our home that should be donated to Deseret Industries. I focused on my task with a vengeance, going through boxes without pausing to get myself or anyone else ready for the day. About eleven o'clock that morning I glanced up momentarily to look at Barbie, then chuckled and questioned aloud, "What's the matter little girl . . . don't you have a Mother?" She was dressed in winter pajama tops (decorated with soft egg yolk from breakfast) and training pants, hobbling along with one bare foot and the other in a red rubber boot she had salvaged from my giveaway box. Her hairdo consisted of yesterday's leftover ponytails. "As soon as I finish this box, I'll get you cleaned up, Barbie. Just be patient." My famous last words stayed in force until about twenty minutes later when a quick headcount revealed Barbie was missing.

She'd never ventured solo outside except a supervised run across the street to play with her friend Kim, so I sent Max Jr. to check at Kim's house while I quickly (thank goodness) got out of my robe and into my clothes for the day. Just as Max Jr. returned with a negative report, a police officer pulled up in front of our home. Imagine my horror to discover his back seat contained my disheveled Barbie (her one boot still fully intact) and her Hot Wheels bike. She had gone on her first unsupervised field trip, nearly making it to the library (about ten blocks away) before her lack of supervision had been noticed and reported. The policeman rolled down his window, asked, "Is that your Mommy?" and with an eager, affirmative nod from Barbie, climbed out to reprimand me. I felt like a two-year-old as he filled out a report.

Later that afternoon, Max returned to a wife who had spent the day in defeated remorse and had made a list of all of the things she couldn't do perfectly. "I can't do it," I sobbed. "I can't even keep track of my children, let alone teach them the things Heavenly Father wants them to know. Everyone else's kids seem to have a good mothers, but your children got stuck with me. We haven't been to the temple for months, Kenny's baby book is blank, and Barbie doesn't even have one. I can't do it all . . . oh, why can't I be like everyone else who seems to be able to handle motherhood with such finesse?"

Believing one must attain perfection is a heavy burden Satan has successfully handed to many Latter-day Saint women. I had accepted his invitation to compare myself to others, subconsciously imagining only a few spaces in the celestial kingdom available to the top contenders. And I didn't see myself close to the top. Several truths discovered since that day have enlarged my myopic view.

1. Life has taught me that Patty Perfect doesn't exist. She is a conglomeration of the best characteristics of many women. She is Sister Christensen's musical family plus Sister Johnson's reverent five-year-old plus Sister Jones' insightful lessons. All of the wonderful traits of all of the wonderful sisters you know both in and out of the Church add up to become Patty Perfect. A careful analysis of each of these sisters individually will show, as President Spencer W. Kimball noted, "They all put their pants on one leg at a time, just like you" (*Church News* [Salt Lake City: Deseret News Publishing Company], 17 Dec. 1988). As you continue with your seasons and growth, part of what makes you special will be added to her magnificence. For now, you are only in competition with your former self, and there is ample room for everyone in the celestial kingdom.

If you don't compare yourself to anyone, how do you know how good you have to be? As long as you are trying your very best, you are as good as you need to be. When Heavenly Father put us on the earth, he never expected us to be perfect. We are imperfect people living in an imperfect world. In fact, he gave us opposition for a reason—that we might learn and grow in our attempt to overcome it.

Our sacrament prayers reflect the expectations and requirements. Every week we hear, "*they are willing* to take upon them the name of thy Son, and always remember him, and keep his commandments which he hath given them" (Moroni 4:3, emphasis added). Nowhere does it ask us to promise to do more than to be willing to try. Brigham Young provides more comforting insight:

> We all occupy diversified stations in the world and in the kingdom of God. Those who do right, and seek the glory of the Father in Heaven, whether their knowledge be little or much, or whether they can do little or much, if they do the very best they know how, they are perfect . . . .
>
> Be ye as perfect as ye can, for that is all we can do though it is written "Be ye perfect as your Father who is in heaven is perfect." To be as perfect as we possibly can according to our knowledge is to be just as perfect as our Father in Heaven is. He cannot be any more perfect than he knows how, any more than we. When we are doing as well as we know in the sphere, and station which we occupy here we are justified . . . we are as justified as the angels who are before the throne of God (*Journal of Discourses*, 2:129–30).

2. A sign posted in my second-grade classroom reminded my students and me, "We don't have to know everything today." Perfection is a lengthy step-by-step process which began in the premortal existence and ends in the world of the hereafter. We are admonished to "continue in patience until ye are perfected" (D&C 67:13). President Spencer W. Kimball remarked: "And how to work toward perfection in our lives? It is not a one-time decision to be made, but a process to be pursued, slowly and laboriously through a lifetime. We build from simple building

blocks, adding refinements as the building rises towards the heavens" (*The Teachings of Spencer W. Kimball,* ed. Edward L. Kimball [Salt Lake City: Bookcraft, 1982], p. 166).

This refinement process takes place in every area of our lives. We can easily see the learning readiness and growth stages of children. The "terrible twos" slip into the "trying threes" as a necessary process that builds step by step. We don't, however, usually acknowledge that a similar process happens to us as we progress through life step by step. We begin every new learning phase with little information, then try, fail or succeed, repent, make adjustments, and try some more. Claudia T. Goates explains this step-by-step process that she has both experienced and observed as it relates to mothering. She feels there are maturing stages of motherhood (infancy, childhood, and adolescence) that we must experience before we reach the maturity phase. These phases are not related to the age of our children, but rather to the process of our learning and growth (see "When You Feel Inadequate as a Mother," *Ensign*, Mar. 1976, pp. 24-25).

As I look back over my growth as a mother, I can also see those same stages of growth. My *infancy* in the mothering experience began as I held a warm, pink bundle and tingled all over as our first daughter, Michelle, looked at me and I looked at her and realized she was my daughter and I was her mother. We began this great adventure together. I had never been a mother before. I naively made my list of things I would never do as a mother and things Michelle would never be allowed to do as my child. I felt prepared; after all, I'd read the books.

My mothering *childhood* brought disconcerting realization that children are individuals who have not read the books. By Michelle's first birthday, Max Jr. was born, necessitating an early graduation of Michelle into a "big girl" bed. We'd go through the routine of saying her prayers, reading a bedtime story, having a drink, and she would still pop out of that bed over and over again. I had read Dr. Spock's book on parenting and knew that he advised against ever shutting a bedroom door on a child. One frustrated evening I decided Dr. Spock couldn't have been as tired as I was when he wrote the book . . . and shut the door. It worked!

I found there were highs (like trying to keep a straight face when asked if we could please plant hotdogs in the garden) and lows (like trying to remove vaseline from the bathroom mirror). But all in all, I loved being a mother, and couldn't understand why anyone would not approve of our beautiful family of four children under the age of five. They were an extension of me, their victories were my victories, their hurts were my hurts.

Shortly thereafter, my mothering *adolescence* began when I was infected with an apparent heart virus that began a year of recovery filled with frustration and learning for our whole family. I cried when my baby cried and I realized I couldn't pick her up. I discovered how ineffective the threat at the end of counting to three became when the children knew I couldn't get off the couch.

The years that followed are a blur. We had McKay in September 1982 and welcomed a beautiful seven-year-old daughter that same December. The highs got more wonderful and the lows soon scraped the bottom of the barrel. I questioned if I could really be the mother Heavenly Father needed me to be. These were my intense learning and refining years when, upon reflection, I learned most of the eternal principles that have brought such peace and happiness to my life today. I would not, however, eagerly line up for a second turn at that period.

My *maturity* phase of motherhood is marked by a calm reassurance that perfection in mothering is a process. I look back over my years as a mother and enjoy the million snapshots taken in my heart of the happy times, and accept the fact that, though far from perfect, I have learned from my mistakes and moved on. I handle current problems by calmly working at them.

I now thoroughly enjoy watching my own children discover how much they are loved as they begin their stages of parenting. My patience with them and others reflects the realization I have that *every* important thread in the tapestry of life (from learning to recite our ABC's to treating others with Christlike charity) follows the same pattern. The beginnings are slow and laborious, the middle seems to take forever, and then the blessings flow.

An envious comparative glance at the blessing phase of another person's life will never take into consideration his or her past developmental steps. We see only the end, missing the faltering steps of the beginning and the long teaching steps of the middle. This can be plainly seen, for example, in the comment of a younger sister in our ward who said, "It would be nice to be like you and not have to get a babysitter every time we want to go out." Her comment totally discounted most of the years since 1973 when we've had to make arrangements for our children at home.

3. We can neither be happy nor effective if we try to be someone besides ourselves. Sister Patricia Holland taught me this truth when she said:

> Our Father in heaven needs us as we are, as we are growing to become. He has intentionally made us different from one another so that even with our imperfections we can fulfill his purposes. My greatest misery comes when I feel I have to fit what others are doing, or what I think others expect of me. I am most happy when I am comfortable being me and trying to do what my Father in heaven and I expect me to be. . . .
>
> . . . We will always have enough resources for being who we are and what we can become.
>
> . . . Each of us will have peace only as we are filling the measure of our *own* creation ("Portraits of Eve," *LDS Women's Treasury* [Salt Lake City: Deseret Book Co., 1997], pp. 97–98, 103).

4. There is a distinct difference between striving for excellence and requiring perfection. Excellence is something every one of us can reach for. Perfection is impossible without the Savior's grace.

It was a cold, blustery day at our cabin in Alpine, Wyoming. The men, including Max Jr., were fishing on the Palisades

Reservoir, and the rest of us had been cooped up all morning. Nerves were running thin. Our five remaining children didn't like the idea that their deer hunt vacation from school was being wasted inside. Finally, about two o'clock in the afternoon, the rain let up. Knowing that all of the adults could use a break, I suggested that the kids (except for Michelle, who was doing homework) bundle up and go down to the lake to see if they could spot our boat and ask how the fishing was going. Everyone jumped at the chance except for Kenny. He wanted to stay and enjoy the warmth of the cabin. I insisted, more for a selfish need for a few minutes of quiet than a prompting.

The prompting, however, did come five minutes later when everyone had gone. "Kenny isn't with them and he needs to go." A quick glance outside showed Kenny standing beside the cabin. After a few minutes of motherly persuasion he was off. Little did I know how important he would be to a successful conclusion to the drama that followed.

It took the little group of four children (Leslie, age 11; Kenny, age 10; Barbie, age 7; and McKay, age 4) only a few minutes to make it down to the shores of the lake. Kenny picked up rocks along the way and kept his favorite ones in his pocket. McKay followed his big brother's example and they both arrived at the lake with pockets bulging.

Having been sternly warned to stay out of the water, and finding no boats within sight, they all four decided to go to the end of the free-floating dock to skip rocks. Kenny was the champion rock skipper, but McKay's lack of mature rock-throwing skills demanded he use his whole body in the effort. A non-related boat passed by the dock and the reverberating waves sent the dock rocking at the same time McKay gave a final, particularly valiant rock-throwing effort, which tumbled him off the dock into the cold, murky water.

The water was about twenty feet deep and Kenny knew his little brother was in trouble. He dove in rocks, coat, shoes and all. He later said, "By the time I got to him, he was about a foot below the water. I didn't know how else to help him, so I dove underneath him and pushed him up to the top of the water to get his breath. When I'd run out of air, I'd go up to the surface and then dive underneath him again until we made it to the dock where Leslie and Barbie pulled him out."

Both boys were freezing, but Kenny refused to put on the girl's coat that was offered. The whole group hurried back to the cabin. McKay (who had been the chosen recipient of both girls' coats) seemed warm enough in his oversized protection, but the other three were shivering uncontrollably. Unaware of their trauma, I chastised them for getting wet and got everyone into a hot shower or bath and then warmed their insides with hot chocolate.

Nothing was said until the following day on our way back home. Then Kenny quietly related, "Mom, I keep thinking about McKay falling into the water yesterday and it scares me." He then recounted the full story. Lying in bed that night, I was overwhelmed with the possibilities of a different outcome. They could have all run for help and we would have lost our youngest son. Kenny could have jumped in and, as is typical of a drowning victim, McKay could have latched on to him, pulling them both under. Kenny was teeny for his age, resulting in only twenty-five pounds difference between the two of them. What made him employ such a novel, safe approach to lifesaving? My conclusion had to be an overwhelming amount of grace. Do we as Latter-day Saints believe in grace? Absolutely! The LDS Bible Dictionary explains:

> [Grace is] a word that occurs frequently in the New Testament, especially in the writings of Paul. The main idea of the word is divine means of help or strength, given through the bounteous mercy and love of Jesus Christ.
> It is through the grace of the Lord Jesus, made possible by his atoning sacrifice, that mankind will be raised in immortality, every person receiving his body from the grave in a condition of everlasting life. It is likewise through the grace of the Lord that individuals, through faith in the atonement of Jesus Christ and

repentance of their sins, receive strength and assistance to do good works that they otherwise would not be able to maintain if left to their own means. This grace is an enabling power that allows men and women to lay hold on eternal life and exaltation after they have expended their own best efforts (s.v. "Grace").

Grace is simply when someone does something for you that you can't do for yourself. McKay couldn't swim, so Kenny, who could swim, saved him. Kenny didn't know how to safely save his brother, so the Spirit prompted him. We can't perfect ourselves, so the Savior, who is perfect, perfects us. Moroni invites:

> Put on thy beautiful garments, O daughter of Zion . . . .
>   Yea, come unto Christ, and be perfected in him, and deny yourselves of all ungodliness; and if ye shall deny yourselves of all ungodliness, and love God with all your might, mind and strength, then is his grace sufficient for you, that by his grace ye may be perfect in Christ; and if by the grace of God ye are perfect in Christ, ye can in nowise deny the power of God.
>   And again, if ye by the grace of God are perfect in Christ, and deny not his power, then are ye sanctified in Christ by the grace of God, through the shedding of the blood of Christ, which is in the covenant of the Father unto the remission of your sins, that ye become holy, without spot (Moroni 10: 31–33).

Sadly, the adversary has whispered directions inviting us to strive to perfect ourselves, leaving the Savior's atonement completely out of the picture. Satan knows perfecting ourselves is an impossible task booby trapped with exploding mines of discouragement and frustration, but many Latter-day Saint women buy in to his plans. Stephen E. Robinson explains that it is one thing to *believe in* Christ, but another to *believe* Christ when he says he can perfect us:

> We all fail at living the full celestial level. That's why we need a Savior. The Lord says, "Blessed are they which do hunger and

thirst after righteousness: for they shall be filled." (Matt. 5:6.) We frequently misinterpret that verse. We think it means "Blessed are the righteous." It does not. When are you hungry? When are you thirsty? When you don't have the object of your desire. It is those who *don't* have the righteousness that God has—*but who hunger and thirst after it*—who are blessed, for if that is the desire of their hearts, the Lord will help them achieve it.

Perfection comes through the atonement of Jesus Christ. That happens as we become one with him, a perfect being.

. . . Many of us are trying to save ourselves, holding the atonement of Jesus Christ at arm's distance and saying, "When I've perfected myself, then I'll be worthy of the Atonement." But that's not how it works. That's like saying, "I won't take the medicine until I'm well. I'll be worthy of it then." . . .

If we will enter into that glorious covenant Jesus offers us and give him all that we have, holding nothing back, trusting in his ability to make up for what we lack, he will exalt us. With him pulling with and for us, we can move forward in confidence toward our celestial home ("Believing Christ," *Ensign*, April 1992, pp. 7–9).

That is the beauty of the Atonement. If we are doing the best we know how, we join hands with our Savior and access the power of the Atonement. Picture yourself struggling to pull the heavy burden of trying to be perfect now. Then the Savior comes and puts his arm around your shoulder. You are yoked together and can pull the burden together until sometime in the eternities when you are strong enough to pull it on your own. Jesus invites us, "Come unto me, all ye that labour and are heavy laden, and I will give you rest. Take my yoke upon you, and learn of me; for I am meek and lowly in heart: and ye shall find rest unto your souls. For my yoke is easy, and my burden is light" (Matthew 11:28-30).

When we have done our best, and have teamed up with the Savior, we can move forward with confidence that all will be well. Joseph Smith received an encouraging revelation: "Therefore, dearly beloved [sisters], let us *cheerfully* do all things that lie in our power; and then may we stand still, with the utmost assurance, to see the salvation of God, and for his arm to be revealed" (D&C 123:17, emphasis added).

Thomas S. Monson has said, "Work without vision is drudgery. Vision without work is dreaming. Work coupled with vision is destiny" ("Keys to Successful Missionary Work," given at New Mission Presidents Seminar, Provo, Utah, 23 June 1987).

Our life could be drudgery without the glorious vision of our future. Remember, "the kingdom of God is within you" (Luke 17:21). Our destiny is exaltation if we continue to try our best, to repent when we fall, and to grow step by step until we receive the fulness of what our Father has to offer. If our vision is firmly fixed on our destiny, one step at a time, day after day, holding hands with the Savior, we can become perfected.

Nay,
Speak No Ill

*T*ROND, A NONMEMBER FOREIGN exchange student from Sweden, was visiting in our home one evening. I had just come home from the hospital after major surgery and he couldn't believe the steady stream of Relief Society sisters. "Here comes another one!" he announced as a hot pot of soup was carried up our driveway. Trond shook his head and grinned, "I've never seen anything like this. It's amazing!"

"This is called the Mormon help hotline," my husband explained. "Our Relief Society ladies can summon dinners in moments when the need arises. They can tell exactly what needs to be done, make calls to a few good sisters, and the need is filled with charity."

When Sister Barbara W. Winder was released as general president of the Relief Society in April conference 1990, she observed, "The work of the Relief Society is focused on the pure and simple part of the gospel, to develop faith and bear testimony; to render compassionate service as we care for the needy; to strengthen our families here and eternally, and to work with our 'hearts knit together in unity and love one towards another.' (Mosiah 18:21)" (*Ensign,* May 1990, p. 76).

"Charity Never Faileth" is our motto. We love our sisters and spend much of our time in compassionate service. But, like every other good thing, the Mormon help hotline has a Satan-inspired flip side. It's called the Mormon gossip line and its fruit is dissension and separation. George Q. Cannon explained the source of anything that divides:

> Whenever the Latter-day Saints become divided; whenever you see one Latter-day Saint arrayed against another, you may know that one or both are in the wrong. When they become divided in their interest, when they seek their own aggrandizement, careless about the rights of their fellowmen; whenever you see this spirit prevail, then it betokens trouble among ourselves and we shall lose power. . . .
>
> And let me say to you, my brethren and sisters, any spirit that leads to division among the Latter-day Saints, you may know is not the Spirit of God; you may know it is from beneath; and if it be evil it will bring destruction upon those who indulge in it (*Collected Discourses,* vol. 1, ed. Brian H. Stuy [Burbank, California, and Woodland Hills, Utah: B.H.S. Publishing, 1987], pp. 349, 350).

The speakers of gossip, hearers of gossip, and subjects of gossip all become victims scattered along the vice's searing path. Surprisingly, the first victim is the speaker of the gossip. A recent article in the *Ensign* explains:

> I hadn't seen Jill for a long time, so although it was storming outside, I decided to pay her a visit. Hoping to avoid the biting wind, I knocked at the side door of her home, which was nearer to my car. She peeked out the window, looked relieved, and quickly let me in.
>
> "Consider yourself privileged," she said. "A few minutes ago, I made a neighbor go around to the front, and the storm was almost as bad as it is now."
>
> "Why?" I asked, surprised because Jill generally goes out of her way to make people feel welcome.
>
> "The last time this neighbor stopped by she told me in detail about the 'despicable state' of someone else's kitchen, right

down to the 'eggshells in the sink'," Jill explained. "I've been involved in about a million projects today, and, well, you can see why there's no way I'm going to let her see this!"

I smiled because her kitchen looked about as lived in as mine sometimes does. "So," she continued, "I made the poor woman endure the storm and go around to my nicely vacuumed front room" (Name Withheld, "The Frigid Wind of Gossip," *Ensign*, Apr. 1998, p. 59).

Every one of us can relate. We have all felt that familiar churn in our stomachs when the doorbell rings in the middle of a di- sas- trous morning the last day of the month and we know it's our vis- iting teachers who will be standing on the front porch. Trust is the key that will decide whether we can have a "move over the laun- dry pile on the couch" visit or a "stay out on the cold porch" visit.

The value of trust is priceless. I taught second grade for ten years. Every year I made a lot of changes in my lesson plans, but plans for the first day always remained intact. I would begin with a subject I thought was the most important lesson they would learn all year. I wanted them to become people that could be trusted. I explained, "A person that can be trusted will always have a job and a wide circle of friends. They will do what is right even though no one is watching. For example, if a person that can be trusted gets hit with a ball during dodgeball, they go out of the circle even if no one else saw the ball touch them. If I need to leave the room, there will be no change in the behavior of people that can be trusted." We did a lot of practicing and talk- ing about the concept because I feel trust is the most important asset anyone can develop. I know Heavenly Father prizes trust. He loves all of his children, but there is only a small percentage of us that he can trust.

Not long ago, an unexpected event reminded me of the secu- rity of being able to trust without reservation. I was tired of answering my phone and having a solicitor waste my time. I trea- sured Monday nights but I thought phone solicitors must have caught on to the fact that a lot of Latter-day Saints are available that night, and doubled their efforts. We bought a Caller ID and started to screen calls. About a week after we got our machine my mom called. She said she had been calling and calling and no one was ever home. I apologized and acknowledged that we weren't home very often, but in my mind I was trying to think of even once that her number had shown up on the Caller ID. I remember thinking, "There must be another explanation. Mom hasn't lied to me in forty-four years. I don't know why she would start today." It was so reassuring knowing I could trust her even though all evidence pointed to a deception. A week later, the phone rang. Max said, "It's a telephone company solicitor." He picked up the phone and said, "Hello" at the same time I said, "Then don't answer it." That particular company had called several times before we bought the Caller ID, and I didn't want to waste any more of their time or mine. Max got the funniest look on his face, looked at me and said, "It's your mother." Apparently, when she used the prefix her telephone company gave her, it appeared on our Caller ID as the telephone company's name and a completely different telephone number. To make things even worse, after hearing the story, our sixteen-year-old son, McKay, said, "I didn't know that number was Grandma. When she kept calling last Thursday, I just kept picking up the receiver and returning it. I must have done that ten times!" I want to be able to be trusted as much as I trusted Mom.

We know that we can trust Heavenly Father and Jesus Christ one hundred percent of the time. When they make a promise, they will always keep it. We know we can trust the prophet. How many of our associates can we absolutely trust?

Larry Hiller, at the time the managing editor of the Church's international magazine, wrote an article about caring for the property of others. He acknowledged that few people treat the tangible property of others with deliberate disregard, but wondered if our integrity extends to less tangible things, such as information. Can we be trustworthy and trust others with information? He likened information to currency:

Many people like to feel and appear important by spending money freely—sometimes going into debt to do so. Similarly, most of us like the feeling of importance that comes from telling others something they did not know. As with money, people may not know we have information unless we "spend," and the temptation to spend can be very powerful. Many of us have had the experience of being in a group where someone relates an interesting piece of information about a person or a forthcoming event. As the discussion progresses, everyone tries to contribute something the others didn't know. It becomes a matter of ego.

At such times, some people give into the temptation to "spend" information they don't have (speculation, rumor, gossip) or, worse yet, to spend information that is not theirs to give by betraying confidences. . . .

When he cannot gain legitimate information, [the "counterfeiter"] simply makes it up. . . .

Just as counterfeit money debases a currency and makes all money suspect, lies and misinformation makes all information suspect. . . .

There are those who cannot abide leaving money in the bank or even in their pocket. If they have it, they must spend it. [The habit] can be disastrous, leading to a poor credit rating and even to bankruptcy.

Most of us have encountered information spendthrifts. . . . Trusting such a person with sensitive information is like entrusting the rent money to a compulsive gambler. . . .

Too many people seem to think that it is only gossip if it is unsubstantiated rumor. But something may be completely true and still be no one else's business. Truth does not justify gossip any more than need justifies theft. And to excuse gossip by saying that it is common knowledge is similar to justifying sin because "others are doing it" ("On Keeping Confidences," *Ensign,* June 1985, pp. 23–24).

Latter-day Saint women have known or have been examples of each of these "spending" types. The sad irony of gossip is that the gossiper figuratively posts a giant neon sign that reads, "Caution, this is not a person you can trust." They tarnish themselves as much as they are tarnishing others. A woman prone to gossip distances herself from close friendships. It doesn't take long to figure out that she who gossips to you will gossip about you.

She judges based only on what she sees and always judges autobiographically, according to her point of view and colored by her experiences. Her point of reference will be completely different than someone else's point of reference because she has been raised a certain way and draws conclusions based on her background. For example, a married college student with no children is in the Relief Society presidency of a married student ward. The other counselor is a married mother who does not attend college, but stays home and takes care of her three-month-old baby. As finals week approaches, the young mother overhears a conversation the student is having with the president. "I'm sorry, but I'm swamped with finals this week. Why don't you ask Melissa if she can be in charge of homemaking. She must have a lot of free time with no classes and only one small baby to take care of."

Don't you think her point of view will dramatically change after the birth of her first baby? Perhaps Jesus' counsel, "in the mouth of two or three witnesses every word may be established" (Matthew 18:16) is fitting in this situation. Combining both or all three points of view will give the bigger picture.

Certain callings in the Church require a strong score of trust. Years ago as a young bishop, my husband was so careful not to divulge anything it seemed like we had to stop communicating. Twenty years later, my older husband as a stake president has sorted out the areas that are out of bounds. Many times people will approach me with, "I don't know what President Molgard has told you—" and I stop them at that point. Max doesn't share any confidential information. His care with others' confidential information has told me that I can safely tell him anything and it won't go any further. Richard P. Lindsay learned a valuable lesson from his father-in-law about Church confidences:

The newly married Lindsays were about to leave on a trip to California when they heard the announcement that their ward was to be divided for the first time in its seventy-five year history. Brother Lindsay's deceased father had been the bishop of the ward for many years, and the young husband felt he had a special interest in what was to take place. But the couple would be out of town and would not be able to learn the details for some time.

Brother Lindsay's father-in-law was serving on the high council at the time, so just before they were due to leave, Brother Lindsay approached the man and asked if he couldn't just whisper the name of the new bishop to them moments before they left. After all, they wouldn't be able to tell anyone else.

The high councilor drew his son-in-law aside and asked with a confidential whisper, "Can you keep a secret?"

"Certainly," the young man assured him.

"Well, so can I." End of conversation. But not the end of the lesson learned.

In a 1980 address to Church employees, Elder Boyd K. Packer spoke admiringly of Elder Joseph Anderson, "who for nearly fifty years was secretary to the First Presidency. He sat with them daily and heard their counseling and made minutes of it all. Fifty years with never a breach of confidence. President David O. McKay said of Joseph Anderson once, 'That man can be quiet in more languages than any man I've known' " (Larry Hiller, "On Keeping Confidences," *Ensign,* June 1985, p. 25).

We have all played the game of trying to figure out who would be the next bishop, Relief Society president, stake president, etc. There always seem to be obvious choices and those names are bantered about in a seemingly innocent speculation game. We are all aware that those leadership positions are chosen by inspiration. There are no signs posted on the lawns of those interested in the calling. There is no debate between candidates. There is no popularity vote. A leader's humble, often lengthy petition through prayer eventually reveals who Heavenly Father wants to serve in that position. Sometimes, however, Heavenly Father chooses an obscure person with a potential not even considered by those not asking in prayer. We need to be aware of the feelings of both those who are issued a call (whose name may not have been mentioned in our guessing game) and those whose names were mentioned in our speculations but were not issued a call. Such speculation could easily tamper with testimonies.

Another problem we encounter is believing in the "only true and living ward." Consider the feelings of those friends divided out of your ward by the ever-growing expansion in Church membership who must now sit as your automatic enemies during road show competition and basketball games.

Ward speculation about why a sister is single, or without children; why her husband doesn't go to church; why her son is straying only results in dividing the flock. Gossip drives people away from each other and Satan is thrilled with the results. There is too much at stake to divide ourselves. Sister Elaine A. Cannon said: "It seems to me that it is time, then, for the women of the Church to behave with a sense of belonging instead of a sense of separateness. We are not women of the world, after all. We are sisters. We are daughters of God. We are children of the covenant who are marching to the same drummer, though we may be singing a separate song" (*Woman to Woman* [Salt Lake City: Deseret Book Co., 1986], p. 66).

Gossiping among members is disheartening, but another deadly form of gossip creeps into our meetings, attitudes, and conversation driving nonmembers and investigators from our Church. Any missionary bringing an investigator worries it might surface. It is a tricky type of gossip that Satan has gently woven into the beautiful fabric of the gospel. It takes gospel truths and weaves them full of pride and exclusion. Many raised in Mormondom overlook or even use this type of gossip, unaware of the departure of the Spirit. I've had its ugly head glare at me countless times. Let me take out my soapbox and explain.

I was raised in a wonderfully stable family. My brother Ted went on a mission to Sweden and all of us, including sisters Vicki,

Kaye, and I have been married in the temple. We went to church every Sunday, even when we were on vacation. Mom took us there. Very few people have the distinction of having a mother who served in a Relief Society presidency at the same time her dad was a lay deacon in the Episcopal Church. I do.

Dad was a remarkable man who did service in his church very much like we do service in ours. He was the executive secretary (senior warden and treasurer) and was in charge of the ward newspaper (Sunday bulletin) for years until they called him to be a counselor in the bishopric (deacon). He visited the shut-ins at least every other Sunday providing the sacrament (Eucharist) to those who were physically unable to attend the church services. He spent countless hours at the cannery (soup kitchen); and raised money for the building fund.

When we were speaking, giving a musical number, or being confirmed in our church, Dad came to give his support. When he entered our church, he seemed to enter with a flourescent sign that declared him a nonmember. Members knew what to do with an investigator sign, but most didn't know how to handle Dad's sign.

Brother Donald Daines was one of the exceptions. He gave more than the usual handshake and "how are you." He realized Dad was so much more than his sign. Brother Daines was our home teacher. He invited us to go water skiing with him in the summer and then invited himself to listen to Dad do some of the readings at the Episcopal Christmas Eve services that we all attended.

When Dad came to our church I'd always pray before we'd go, "Please help Dad to feel the Spirit and be touched today." Mom was the Primary chorister and I watched Dad shed tears during the sacrament meeting programs. Most of the time, though, he'd come for fast and testimony meetings. That's where the problem he had faced growing up in Salt Lake City would be most likely to surface. Someone inevitably gossiped about his church over the pulpit.

While you swallow your gasps, let's set the stage a little more in line to your understanding. Let's pretend that you somehow got the privilege of bringing Mother Theresa to fast and testimony meeting. A more saintly woman could not be found in or out of the Church. Someone doesn't see that she is in attendance and the spirit of love is interrupted by the following words:

"I'd like to bear my testimony. I know this Church is true. Jesus Christ is the head of our church. I'm glad I don't belong to another church. It would be sad to be part of the great and abominable church spoken of in the Book of Mormon. Satan is in charge of other churches. I'm glad that we have a prophet so we're not led astray like they are."

Following that fiasco, invite her to Sunday School class where you might hear comments such as, "Priests in other religions wouldn't stay if they didn't get paid. They're just in it for the money."

Over the years, I sat next to Daddy in meeting after meeting listening to comments like these. They were not edifying words, although those encased in the Mormon cocoon don't hear how self-righteous they sound. Elevating ourselves while saying derogatory remarks about someone else is gossip. The setting and motive are irrelevant. President Gordon B. Hinckley voiced his concerns and cautions in April 1998 at general conference:

> This is [the Lord's] unique and wonderful cause. We bear testimony and witness of Him. But we need not do so with arrogance or self-righteousness. . . .
>
> A holier-than-thou attitude is not becoming to us. . . .
>
> Let us rise above all such conduct and teach our children to do likewise. Let us be true disciples of the Christ, observing the Golden Rule, doing unto others as we would have them do unto us. Let us strengthen our own faith and that of our children while being gracious to those who are not of our faith. Love and respect will overcome every element of animosity. Our kindness may be the most persuasive argument for that which we believe (*Ensign*, May 1998, p. 5).

The tone of condescending words brings negative feelings. How different Dad's visit could have been if he would have heard words similar to those spoken by President Spencer W. Kimball: "We say to our friends of the world, we love and admire you. We are grateful for your resolve to be righteous in an increasingly wicked world. Bring all that you have that is good and wholesome with you, and let us add to all that you have, that which we have—the fullness of the gospel and the even greater blessings that can follow unto you through membership in The Church of Jesus Christ of Latter-day Saints!" (*The Teachings of Spencer W. Kimball*, ed. Edward L. Kimball [Salt Lake City: Bookcraft, 1982], p. 552).

Remember, nonmembers also have and must fill the important measure of their creation. Elder Ezra Taft Benson's words may expand our view:

> God, the Father of us all, uses the men of the earth, especially good men [and women], to accomplish his purposes. It has been true in the past, it is true today, it will be true in the future.
>
> "Perhaps the Lord needs such men on the outside of His Church to help it along," said the late Orson F. Whitney of the Quorum of the Twelve. "They are among its auxiliaries and can do more for the cause where the Lord has placed them, than anywhere else . . . . Hence, some are drawn into the fold and receive a testimony of the truth; while others remain unconverted . . . the beauties and glories of the gospel being veiled temporarily from their view, for a wise purpose. The Lord will open their eyes in His own due time. God is using more than one people for the accomplishment of His great and marvelous work. The Latter-day Saints cannot do it all. It is too vast, too arduous for any one people . . . . We have no quarrel with the gentiles. They are partners in a certain sense." (Conference Report, Apr. 1928, p. 59.) (Conference Report, April 1972, p. 49).

It has been my observation that a sister who removes the blight of gossip from her life generally goes through three stages:

Stage 1: She relishes gossip and feels her own importance is a reflection on the fact that others call her to report any new tidbit. In a reciprocation of their friendship, she always feels it her duty to add some information to the conversation. She is, as one book reviewer described, "radiant with sorrow" at others misfortunes. She would never tell a flat-out lie, but may increasingly become color-blind as the little white lies are stretched to embellish. If she becomes the victim of the gossip, she feels she needs to call everyone she knows to make sure they don't believe the story and to gather as many people as she can to stand on her side of the battle. She is sadly unaware of the damage she is causing.

Stage one people have been a perpetual problem in God's kingdom. Think what happened to the Prophet Joseph Smith because of gossip. Think what happened to the Savior because of gossip. Jesus taught his disciples, "Do not ye yet understand, that whatsoever entereth in at the mouth goeth into the belly, and is cast out into the draught? But those things which *proceed out of the mouth come forth from the heart*, and they defile the man" (Matthew 15:17-18, emphasis added).

The strength of our character and testimony, what is in our heart, is reflected in what we speak. Brigham Young contended this was true when he said, "If there is nothing in the heart which governs us, and controls to an evil effect, the tongue of itself will never produce evil. Words do not spring spontaneously into existence; they are a product of our very natures. Good words issue from goodness in the heart, evil words from evil in the heart" (quoted in the *Church News,* May 11, 1991).

Larry Hiller adds, "Unfortunately, the word *gossip* is like the word *repentance*. Those who most need to hear it immediately retreat behind a wall of rationalization. That is one of the major problems with gossip: it is so easily rationalized. When others do it, it is gossip. When I do it we are merely discussing someone else in friendly conversation" (*Ensign,* June 1985, p. 25).

And Spencer J. Condie says, "Hugh Nibley once remarked

that 'a shabby substitute for repentance is to compare our life with someone wickeder than we are' " (*Your Agency: Handle with Care* [Salt Lake City: Bookcraft, 1996], p. 25).

Sisters in stage one are Satan's handmaidens in the Relief Society organization. When Satan cannot keep her from visiting teaching, he gets her to taint the visit with gossip. The good of her compassionate service is darkened because she brings gossip in one hand and a pot of soup in the other.

Stage 2: Fortunately, life is a strict teacher. Somewhere along the path of life, the talebearer is caught in her own snare. She may have a difficult time with a wayward child. Her "friends" listen and soon her troubles are broadcast throughout the city. Or perhaps she finds herself in a situation like one told of by Elder Gene R. Cook:

> Solemnly, people began to gather outside the mission president's office. Exchanging astonished glances, many could still not believe that they had been summoned to a church court. The officers of the court were full of love and understanding, but very serious in the investigation of the charges; those present could lose their membership in the The Church of Jesus Christ of Latter-day Saints. The charge was not immorality or apostasy; they were accused of speaking evil of a neighbor.
>
> A fine brother had been slandered by those gathered together that evening, accused of the serious charge of immorality. He was completely innocent, but the great damage that had been done by "those whom he counted as his friends" would not be easily repaired. Who could measure the near destruction of this good soul? Who could measure the impact on the branch, as its fellowship was eroded? And what about the effect on those nonmembers who also became involved? Who could ever undo the evil that had affected hundreds of lives?
>
> It had happened so easily. It began with simple words like—
> "Did you hear . . .?"
> "Sister Joan said . . ."
> "I have heard that he told her . . ."
> "I am not sure about this . . ."

"If you won't repeat this, I guess I could tell you that . . ."
("Gossip, Satan's Snare," *Ensign*, Jan. 1981, p. 27).

Somehow, she feels the pain she has been causing. Somehow,
life hits her with a true picture of the damaging effects of gossip.

Stage 3: After asking for forgiveness from the Lord, who suf-
fered for her transgression, she goes through her life with a fine-
toothed comb and tries to repair the damage that she has caused.
She realizes the truth of the sayings, "you can't get the tooth-
paste back into the tube" and "gathering the dandelion fluff after
it has been blown is impossible."

She then strives to follow the pattern set by the Lord in Doctrine and Covenants 136:24: "Let your words tend to edifying
one another." Words that edify bring the light of Christ, and are
productive and useful. Before she speaks, she asks, "What is my
motive? Will my words help to build up the kingdom?"

Because Satan's domain is so prevalent, the stage three sister
will find herself rubbing shoulders with stage one sisters. Elder
Neal A. Maxwell advises: "While we are not always free to choose
just when and how all of life's interactions will occur, we are nevertheless free to choose our responses to these moments. Since
we can't compute beforehand all our responses—there may be no
time in which to ponder how we will respond—it becomes vital
to set our course as immortals on the basis of immortal principles
applied as reflexively as possible" ("The Pathway to Discipleship," *Ensign*, Sept. 1998, p. 10).

Our stage three sister realizes that "where no wood is, there
the fire goeth out: so where there is no talebearer, the strife
ceaseth" (Proverbs 26:20). Instead of adding fuel to the negative
fire, she tries to squelch it by making a charitable contribution, a
reminder of the good qualities of the person, or she offers
another possible point of view, then excuses herself and carries
the information no further.

She carefully safeguards her private troubles. Needing to talk
to someone, she looks for someone she can trust. Those who
gossip are automatically eliminated from her list. She chooses to

counsel with a spouse or other family member, a bishop, or a trustworthy close friend who speaks of topics besides others' difficulties. The sharing time is treasured as she unburdens her problems, looking for productive solutions. The Spirit is present and she knows their conversation will be carefully safeguarded by her confidant.

There is power for families, the gospel, and the community in her unifying qualities. I saw a wonderful example of that kind of oneness nearly ten years ago. Dad contracted a particularly fast-moving cancer that took him from a healthy man at Christmas to terrific pain through the month of January and finally to hospitalization in February that lasted only a week. Members of our church rallied around our entire family. Episcopal priests, other deacons, and even the Bishop of Utah came to visit Dad at the hospital. Some came many times even though we were many miles from where they lived. They brought such a beautiful spirit of love. We held hands around Dad's bed as they prayed for him and the spiritual feeling was peaceful and strong.

When Dad died, the members of both congregations poured into Mom's home. They brought food and tender concern and filled her home with the kind of love that tore down "nonmember" signs on both sides. Dad, of course, had wanted an Episcopal service, but Mom needed consolation from her church also. Our fears of hurting the members of either denomination were quickly put to rest.

It was a beautiful service, with Dad's church full of Latter-day Saints and Episcopalians sitting side by side. His grandchildren sang "I Am a Child of God" and a copy was requested afterwards by the Episcopal children's choir director. Max spoke as a representative of our family, carefully avoiding any comments that didn't edify.

The church was full of members of the Episcopal priesthood in their white robes. They conducted the services. The last song was a favorite of Dad's called "Hold High the Cross." It was a beautiful song, and I thought I heard the angels chime in on the last verse. Dad was buried in the deacon's robe that he was so proud of.

The dinner after the services was a combined effort of our Relief Society ladies and the Episcopal ladies. They had coordinated the effort so that everyone could help. I sat back and thought of the many gifts that Dad had given me and knew that one of the best gifts that I have is the gift of love for people who are not members of our church. His funeral was a testimony of what we had lived: we are all children of God.

Cheryl B. Preston reminds us:

> Our code as Christian soldiers, our handbook of instructions, is the scriptures. They reverberate with pleas for solidarity and refraining from judgment. They urge us to seek the unity that underlies a Zion society. (4 Nephi 1:17; Moses 7:18.) They remind, "Every [sisterhood] divided against itself is brought to desolation; and a house divided against a house falleth." (Luke 11:17; see also Mark 3:24-25; Matthew 12:25.) As sisters in the gospel, we have promised to bear one another's burdens, not increase them. (Mosiah 18:8; Galatians 6:2.) Moreover, we have been told by "Christ, the royal Master, / [who] Leads against the foe" (*Hymns of The Church of Jesus Christ of Latter-day Saints* [Salt Lake City: The Church of Jesus Christ of Latter-day Saints, 1985], no. 246), that, if we are not one, we are not his. (D&C 38:27.) (*Women in the Covenant of Grace: Talks Selected from the 1993 Women's Conference,* ed. Dawn Hall Anderson and Susette Fletcher Green [Salt Lake City: Deseret Book Co., 1994], p. 183).

The book of Jude speaks of some in the last days who separate themselves, because they don't have the Spirit. It also says there will be some who have compassion and will make a difference (see Jude 1:18-22). The difference will be unity. One by one, as we work to squelch the ugly blight of gossip in our lives and the lives of our families, wards, and communities, we will make a difference.

Lucy Mack Smith's words, found in the minutes of one of the first Relief Society meetings, tell us how that unity will happen.

Her inspired words echo down the chambers of time and invite sisters today to follow her example: "We must cherish one another, watch over one another, comfort one another, and gain instruction, that we may all sit down in heaven together" (Relief Society Minutes of Nauvoo, Mar. 24, 1842, LDS Church Archives).

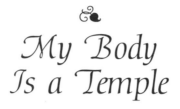

My Body
Is a Temple

$\mathcal{T}$AKE A PEEK AT YOURSELF BACK in the far reaches of pre-earth life. Who were you? You began as spiritual intelligence. Joseph Smith taught that this spiritual element has always existed; it is co-eternal with God (see *Teachings of the Prophet Joseph Smith*, [Salt Lake City: Deseret Book Co., 1938], pp. 352–54). Somehow, that spiritual material was used to form everything spiritual.

Everything alive on the earth was created spiritually before it was created physically. There were spirit plants, spirit chickens, spirit fishes, and spirit trees. We were created as spiritual sons and daughters, offspring of a Heavenly Father and Heavenly Mother. Our spiritual body of the premortal existence must have looked very much like our temporal body. Parley P. Pratt explained, "The spirit of man consists of an organization of the elements of spiritual matter in the likeness and after the pattern of the fleshly tabernacle. It possesses, in fact, all the organs and parts exactly corresponding to the outward tabernacle" (*Key to the Science of Theology*, 10th ed. [Salt Lake City: Deseret Book Co., 1948], p. 79). In that wonderful spiritual family, Jesus Christ was our eldest brother.

The brother of Jared was allowed to see what a spirit body looks like. He was allowed the glorious opportunity of seeing

Jesus before He was born and was told, "Behold, this body, which ye now behold, is the body of my spirit; and man have I created after the body of my spirit; and even as I appear unto thee to be in the spirit will I appear unto my people in the flesh" (Ether 3:16).

We learned and progressed in that spiritual realm. We had free agency there and it was a time of schooling and probation. Some eventually exercised their agency to become fallen followers of Lucifer, which meant that was the end of their progression. They would never get a mortal body or have children, which is really good news. We have enough problems without Satan and his kingdom multiplying and replenishing. Some righteous spirits not only chose to follow God's firstborn, they progressed enough to earn the right to be one of the noble and great, fore-ordained to lead and do the work of the Lord on earth. We shouted for joy in anticipation of the opportunity to clothe our spirits in mortal bodies. We would be put into families according to our righteousness in the premortal existence. President Harold B. Lee explained, "You are now born into a family to which you have come, into the nations through which you have come, as a reward for the kind of lives you lived before you came here and at a time in the world's history, as the Apostle Paul taught the men of Athens and as the Lord revealed to Moses, determined by the faithfulness of each of those who lived before this world was created" (*Ensign*, Jan. 1974, p. 5).

Heavenly Father wanted our growth and learning to continue in mortality. The veil was drawn, agency and opposition were established, and we eagerly anticipated our turn on earth. It must have seemed like our turn would never come as we waved good-bye to the millions born before us. Finally, an infant wail announced our birth into mortality as we became a living soul, our body and spirit joined together for our entire mortal existence. Our jerky movements broadcast the newness of the experience. We weren't good at anything except having our body demand what it needed.

I work one day a week at the obstetrics wing of a hospital. I feel much like a veil worker as I watch the miracle of birth. The new mother soon discovers that her training in charity begins as her desires take a back seat to the baby's needs. I've never heard a baby say, "What can I do to help you?" No, their demanding cries focus all the attention on what they need. They need to be selfish so their physical needs are met.

Living in this age with the knowledge of the restored gospel available to us tells us we made a lot of good decisions in the premortal existence. Satan didn't like us then and he certainly noted our birth. As we grow, we are given a spiritual head start, so to speak. Satan may have noted our birth but the rule is he has to leave us alone for eight years. The Lord says that "power is not given unto Satan to tempt little children, until they begin to become accountable before me" (D&C 29:47). We hope that the instructions of righteous parents and teachers plant strong seeds of integrity that will be able to conquer the heinous influence that is allowed to attack when we arrive at the age of account-ability and are back in Satan's day planner.

Those preaccountability years mark the inauguration of our attempts to control and master our new body. We soon discov-ered that both our spirit and our body have appetites. Those appetites come from two different sources. Elder Melvin J. Bal-lard clarified:

> All the assaults that the enemy of our souls will make to capture us will be through the flesh, because it is made up of the unre-deemed earth, and he has power over the elements of the earth. The approach he makes to us will be through the lusts, the appetites, the ambitions of the flesh. All the help that comes to us from the Lord to aid us in this struggle will come to us through the spirit that dwells within this mortal body. So these two mighty forces are operating upon us through these two channels. . . .
>
> I said that the assault that the evil one will make upon us to capture us will be made through the body. That is the line of contact. You have all heard the adage that a chain is no stronger

than its weakest link. It will break at its weak point. Generally we will observe that our weak link is in the flesh. The devil knows the weak link, and when he undertakes to capture a soul he will strike at the weak point. There may be strength elsewhere, but he never attacks us where we are strong. He attacks where we are weak. . . .

It is not bodies, it is immortal spirits that the devil wants. And he tries to capture them through the body, for the body can enslave the spirit, but the spirit can keep the body a servant and be its master ("Struggles for the Soul," *The New Era,* Mar. 1984, pp. 35–37).

Satan thinks the body is his realm. The Apostle Paul shed new light on that lie when he said, "Know ye not that ye are the temple of God, and that the Spirit of God dwelleth in you? If any man defile the temple of God, him shall God destroy; for the temple of God is holy, which temple ye are" (1 Corinthians 3:16–17).

A temple is a holy, sacred place where revelation can be received. It can be consecrated (set apart as holy) to do the work of the Lord. The decision to consecrate our body to his work is left to our agency. We can take into our bodies whatever we choose.

Hezekiah was the King of Judah (the southern kingdom) about 701 B.C. His father, Ahaz, was a wicked king who had desecrated the temple of the Lord. The first month of his reign, Hezekiah opened the doors of the temple, brought in the priests and the Levites and said, "Hear me, ye Levites, . . . sanctify the house of the Lord God of your fathers, and carry forth the filthiness out of the holy place" (2 Chronicles 29:5).

When all that didn't belong in the temple was taken out, and all the things that did belong in the temple were brought back in, the temple again became a place to prepare chosen people to come into the presence of the Lord and be like him.

We can have a like experience in cleaning the temple that houses our spirit. Elder Russell M. Nelson explained:

When we understand our nature and our purpose on earth, and that our bodies are physical temples of God, we will realize that it is sacrilege to let anything enter the body that might defile it. It is irreverent to let even the gaze of our precious eyesight or the sensors of our touch or hearing supply the brain with memories that are unclean or unworthy. . . .

When we truly know our divine nature, we will want to control our appetites. We will focus our eyes on sights, our ears on sounds, and our minds on thoughts that are a credit to our physical creation as a temple of our Father in Heaven ("The Magnificence of Man," *Ensign*, Jan. 1988, pp. 68–69).

Some of the addictions of the flesh are pointed out specifically in the Word of Wisdom. Latter-day Saint women strive not to smoke, drink alcohol, tea, or coffee. These are the letter of the law. A careful, prayerful, and personal study will bless us with the spirit of the law as it relates to us. Keep in mind the spirit will not prompt you to be fanatical. Satan can and does cause Latter-day Saint women and their spouses to concentrate on their interpretation of the Word of Wisdom so fanatically that it becomes their whole gospel.

Elder Boyd K. Packer likened the fulness of the gospel to a piano keyboard. He explained that a person could be "attracted by a single key," [such as keeping the Word of Wisdom] he or she wants to hear "played over and over again." He continued: "Some members of the Church who should know better pick out a hobby key or two and tap them incessantly, to the irritation of those around them. They can dull their own spiritual sensitivities. They lose track that there is a fulness of the gospel . . . [which they reject] in preference to a favorite note. This becomes exaggerated and distorted, leading them away into apostasy" ("The Only True and Living Church," *Ensign*, Dec. 1971, p. 42).

Examining and cleansing our bodily temples of those things in which our physical body is controlling or inhibiting our spirit will bring rich temporal and spiritual blessings. Many types of addictions can waste precious time and money and can divert our attention away from the Savior. What things might be in that category? Elder Russell M. Nelson suggests that "if you yield to anything that can addict, and thus defy the Word of Wisdom, your spirit surrenders to the body. The *flesh* then enslaves the *spirit*" ("Self-Mastery," *Ensign*, Nov. 1985, p. 31). Are you keeping the Word of Wisdom and receiving the full benefit of the blessings promised therein?

All we need to do is to ask of our Father in Heaven what needs to be cleansed from our temple. "And if men come unto me I will show unto them their weakness. . . . For if they will humble themselves before me, and have faith in me, then will I make weak things become strong unto them" (Ether 12:27).

A short list of items that might be problematic to Latter-day Saint women may include an inordinate amount of time or lack of quality restraints on television, movies, or the Internet, and addictions to shopping, food, or prescription drugs. These problems can begin inside the circle of normal and even righteous motives. Elder Joseph B. Wirthlin explains:

> While traveling along a mountainous road one evening through a driving rainstorm punctuated with frequent claps of thunder and flashes of lightning, Sister Wirthlin and I could barely see the road, either in front of us or to the right and the left. I watched the white lines on that road more intently than ever before. Staying within the lines kept us from going onto the shoulder and into the deep canyon on one side and helped us avoid a head-on collision on the other. To wander over either line could have been very dangerous. Then I thought, "Would a right-thinking person deviate to the left or the right of a traffic lane if he knew the result would be fatal? If he valued his mortal life, certainly he would stay between these lines."
>
> That experience traveling on this mountain road is so like life. If we stay within the lines that God has marked, he will protect us, and we can arrive safely at our destination. . . .
>
> We get sidetracked by submitting to temptations that divert us past the bounds of safety. Satan knows our weaknesses. He

puts attractive snares on our paths at just those moments when we are most vulnerable. His intent is to lead us from the way that returns us to our Heavenly Father. Sin may result from activities that begin innocently or that are perfectly legitimate in moderation, but in excess, they can cause us to veer from the straight and narrow path to our destruction ("The Straight and Narrow Way," *Ensign*, Nov. 1990, pp. 64–65).

Satan's cruel deceptions are so discreet. If an addiction is holding you captive, I know it began innocently. A prescription drug for physical or emotional pain; food that soothes; credit spending; Internet chatting—the list goes on and on. That initial, innocent beginning gave you a feeling of well-being or euphoria. Physical or emotional pain such as tension, loneliness, inadequacy, or fear were temporarily lost in that initial effect. When they returned, your mind remembered and you tried it again. That good feeling continued.

Whatever your addiction or craving, it probably started as a minor infraction. The demand could be likened to a butterfly, whose presence you may have noticed, but which seemed to present no threat. As your mind and body developed a tolerance for this presence, you eventually ceased to recognize its existence. The addiction soon demanded more substance to fill its desire. You needed more spending, more prescription drug, more food. That tiny, unobtrusive butterfly soon became more like a barking dog. The needs of the addiction became more pointed, like a dog the cravings barked and barked until they were fed. Once the substance was provided, the barking stopped and your peace and euphoria could return.

As time passed the addiction required more and more of you. Eventually, so slowly that you hardly noticed, the dog was replaced by a ravenous tiger. The addiction now overpowered you. How, you wondered, could what seemed as innocent and inconspicuous as a butterfly become such a terrible beast? Sadly, such addictions feed themselves. As each demand is satisfied, a new demand is made.

Unfortunately, many caught in this terrible cycle see the cause of the problem—the addiction itself—as the only means of escape. To avoid the pain of the destructive pattern, they feed the addiction in an attempt to find euphoria. Through this process self-esteem is diminished and personal spirituality declines.

Even good things can be taken to extremes and become vices leading to possible addictions. As long as we entertain those addictions and carnal desires, we are in Satan's bondage. Elder Robert L. Backman explained a type of bondage when he told the following story:

> In Africa, the natives have a unique, effective way to capture monkeys. They lop the top off a coconut, remove the meat, and leave a hole in the top of the coconut large enough for the monkey to put his paw in. Then they anchor the coconut to the ground with some peanuts in it. When the natives leave, the monkeys, smelling those delicious peanuts, approach the coconuts, see the peanuts in them, put their paws in to grasp the nuts, and attempt to remove the nuts—but find that the hole is too small for their doubled-up fists. The natives return with gunny sacks and pick up the monkey—clawing, biting, screaming—but they won't drop the peanuts to save their lives ("To the Young Men of the Church," *Ensign*, Nov. 1980, p. 42).

Are we clinging to "peanuts" that keep us miserable? Remember Nephi who asked: "Why should I yield to sin, because of my flesh? Yea, why should I give way to temptations, that the evil one have place in my heart to destroy my peace and afflict my soul?" (2 Nephi 4:27). This great prophet recognized the snares of the adversary, baited with so many temptations: "Nevertheless, notwithstanding the great goodness of the Lord, in showing me his great and marvelous works, my heart exclaimeth: O wretched man that I am! Yea, my heart sorroweth because of my flesh and my soul grieveth because of mine iniquities. I am encompassed about, because of the temptations and the sins which do so easily beset me" (2 Nephi 4:17-18).

Often these sins that so easily beset us elicit many excuses. "My body just naturally craves sugary (or high fat) foods." "I shop out of control because of what is going on in my life. It soothes my problems." "I started taking that drug because of depression, (pain, anxiety . . .) and now the prescribed amount doesn't work. My doctor doesn't understand. I need more than he will give me."

Each of us is susceptible to various feelings and impulses. President Boyd K. Packer has indicated that "some are worthy and some of them are not; some of them are natural and some of them are not." Regardless of the nature or source of our mortal urges, President Packer makes it clear that "we are to control them" ("Covenants," *Ensign,* Nov. 1990, p. 85).

In his April 1990 conference address, Elder Richard G. Scott gave a beautiful talk entitled "Finding the Way Back." Some of the highlights include:

> Lucifer will do all in his power to keep you captive. You are familiar with his strategy. He whispers: "No one will ever know." "Just one more time." "You can't change; you have tried before and failed." "It's too late; you've gone too far." Don't let him discourage you. . . .
>
> If you've tangled your ordered life into a ball of knots, it has taken time to get it that way. It is unreasonable to expect to unravel it all at once. Start knot by knot, decision by decision, and be sure that while you are untying the knots, you don't let any more get put there through transgression. . . .
>
> . . . Decide to stop what you are doing that is wrong. Then search out everything in your life that feeds the habit, such as negative thoughts, unwholesome environment, and your companions in mischief. Systematically eliminate or overcome everything that contributes to that negative part of your life. Then stop the negative things permanently.
>
> Recognize that you'll go through two transition periods. The first is the most difficult. You are caging the tiger that has controlled your life. It will shake the bars, growl, threaten, and

cause you some disturbance. But I promise you that this period will pass. How long it takes will depend upon the severity of your transgression, the strength of your determination, and the help you seek from the Lord. But remember, as you stand firm, it will pass.

The second period is not as intense. It is like being on "battle alert" so that you can fend off any enemy attack. That, too, will pass, and you will feel more peace and will have increased control of your life. You will become free. . . .

Some days are more difficult than others, but the process becomes easier because through your use of agency, you qualify for the Lord's help and He magnifies your efforts. (See Omni 1:26.) (*Ensign,* May 1990, pp. 74–75).

Jesus Christ with his Atonement is the essential piece that is so often left out of our quest for physical mastery. We run here after medication and there after programs, paying great sums of money to find the answer. We are after self-control, recognizing we must first do all that is within our power. We spend numerous hours on our knees praying that we will have self-control. Overcoming our weaknesses in this way leaves us likening ourselves to the people in Helaman: "And because of . . . their boastings in their own strength, they were left in their own strength; therefore they did not prosper" (Helaman 4:13).

When we discover we can't do it on our own, we begin the cycle of despair: wallowing in self-pity, making new resolutions, having self-control for short periods and falling again. As we follow the cycle we are ever watchful of that new program that will give us the control we are looking for. Without the Savior programs won't help, no matter how expensive they are, how many studies back them up, or how successful others have been using them. Every recovery program speaks of turning our lives over to a greater Power who can remove all shortcomings. As Latter-day Saints we recognize that Power to be our Savior.

The difference between the Savior's recovery program is that the worldly recovery programs work from the outside, on your mortal body. We were created spiritually first and temporally second. To successfully overcome our weaknesses, we must improve in that same order. This is the true order for every problem we encounter in life. Again, in the language of President Ezra Taft Benson: "The Lord works from the inside out. The world works from the outside in. The world would take people out of the slums. Christ takes the slums out of people, and then they take themselves out of the slums. The world would mold men by changing their environment. Christ changes men, who then change their environment. The world would shape human behavior, but Christ can change human nature" ("Born of God," *Ensign*, July 1989, p. 4).

How will he do it? Several steps will be necessary:

1. *Recognize that the Savior created everything and everyone, worlds without end.* He knows all things, and has power over all things. Every cell, every atom, every ion is under his control.

2. *Accept the fact that we will never be perfect without our Savior's grace and mercy.* A certain young woman named Sarah had been raised in the Church with the multiple blessings of the gospel. Those blessings included worthy parents who chose to have a large family and a stay-at-home mother. Sarah loved her brothers and sisters but could hardly wait to get out on her own where she could feel free of her parents' scrimp and save mentality. Her dreams included a job with enough money to spend as she pleased. Her older brother had gone to medical school and she secretly envied his nice home and his wife's seemingly unending supply of clothing, furniture, and shoes! Why, Sarah was convinced that Brittany could go for years without wearing the same pair twice.

A college scholarship offered the opportunity Sarah had been waiting for. She listened to last-minute cautions from her mother about being careful with money, rolled her eyes, and said good-bye to her financially-restricted former life. It was exhilarating to be old enough to be an adult in an adult world—to be free, finally.

Sarah truly felt adult. She had already made a decision that her mother didn't know about. Several credit card companies had sent her offers of credit and she had applied for them. Now she would have the freedom to spend without mom and dad looking over her shoulder. How else would she be able to establish credit for herself? It really was a puzzle to her why her mom thought credit cards were a problem. The low monthly payments could easily be taken care of with her part-time job at the bookstore.

Sarah's first few weeks were truly glorious. She bought a whole new wardrobe and finally looked, she thought, like everyone else. Her shoes matched, her jewelry matched, and her makeup matched. An expensive makeover at the mall had resulted in a new hairdo that completed her perfect look. Friends admired her things and she bought gifts to enrich their friendships. She had topped out some of her cards, but others had sent offers and she still had a few she hadn't even used. She reasoned that the minimum payments were low and when she finished school and got a real job she could easily pay it all back.

Unfortunately, the glory of her shopping soon began to fade as the creditors started calling. Promises of "it's in the mail" and "I'll pay that next week" weren't accepted as readily as they had been initially. Her phone was ringing incessantly. She felt she had no choice but to get an answering machine and try to put those angry voices out of her mind. Who did they think they were trying to invade her life?

Letters came warning of court actions. Sarah paid what she could but threw most of the letters away. Fines and interest piled up until she had dug herself a hole she couldn't possibly get out of. A court date was set.

The judge shook his head and said, "Sarah, taking things without paying for them is stealing. Justice must be served! Those you owe must be paid! Unless you can come up with the money now, I will have no choice but to put you behind bars."

In tears, Sarah pled with the judge. Didn't he have any mercy? In answer to her plea, the gavel came down with a resounding thud that echoed through the room. "Justice must be served!" The long silence was broken only by Sarah's muffled sobs of complete despair.

The sound of a shuffle and then hurried footsteps filled the room. A familiar voice said, "Judge, what if I pay her debts. Will that satisfy justice?" It was her older brother. "I know Sarah has made many serious mistakes. She will have to quit school for a while and can work in my office full-time while she lives in our home. It won't be easy, but I know with my help, she can turn her life around."

The judge thoughtfully nodded. Yes, justice would be served as her debtors would be paid. Sarah's youth and inexperience allowed for mercy. Both laws were satisfied.

The Savior is our older brother who stands both willing and able. Alma 42:22-24 states:

> But there is a law given, and a punishment affixed, and a repentance granted; which repentance, mercy claimeth; otherwise, justice claimeth the creature and executeth the law, and the law inflicteth the punishment; if not so, the works of justice would be destroyed, and God would cease to be God.
>
> But God ceaseth not to be God, and mercy claimeth the penitent, and mercy cometh because of the atonement. . . .
>
> For behold, justice exerciseth all his demands, and also mercy claimeth all which is her own; and thus, none but the truly penitent are saved.

I once heard a statement that says it all: He paid a debt he didn't owe because we had a debt we couldn't pay.

3. *Be willing to give the Savior all.* C. S. Lewis put it beautifully when he said, "Christ says, 'Give me all. I don't want so much of your time and so much of your money and so much of your work: I want You. I have not come to torment your natural self, but to kill it. No half-measures are any good. I don't want to cut off a branch here and a branch there, I want to have the whole tree down. . . . Hand over the whole natural self, all the desires which you think innocent as well as the ones you think wicked—the whole outfit. I will give you a new self instead. In fact, I will give you Myself: my will shall become yours' " (*Mere Christianity* [New York: Collier books, 1960], p. 167).

The only thing we have total control over is our agency. The key to overcoming our addictions lies in our submission to our Master's will. When your will becomes his will, you can pray continuously throughout the day, "Jesus, Savior, pilot me." With full repentance, humility, and faith in his powers you can ask, "Lord, what will thou have me to do?" and he will pilot you. When he answers through the spirit, follow that answer. It will lead you to a point where you will eventually have no desire to do evil.

I have had the glorious opportunity of tasting, for a time, the sweetness of the experience of having no desire to do evil. Elder Russell M. Nelson called and set apart my husband to be the president of the Tooele Stake. The new stake presidency and their wives were given the wonderful privilege of spending lunch and a session of training that afternoon with Elder Nelson. I came out of that training session somehow changed. I had spent time with someone so close to the Savior that somehow he had shared his glowing countenance. I had no disposition to do evil. Just as the disciples who had personally been with Christ were changed, I understood that change. I stayed clear of the television for fear it would taint that feeling. I didn't want to hear gossip, be around any contention, or let the world into my haven. I wanted that feeling to continue.

It did continue for several days and then the world invaded my turf. I retained pieces, but the whole pie is being dished out to me piecemeal as I grow and learn. I do possess a remembrance of that feeling and have recently discovered that as I allow the Savior to lead me in my decisions, my actions, my thoughts, yes, even my life, the temporal challenges depart. When I concentrate on that power, a power greater than any demonic power, the tempting voices within are stilled. My life, though still far from perfect, is heading in the right direction. That power is offered to all. We will all achieve self-mastery when we turn ourselves over to the Master.

&

"I Have
Overcome the World"

$\mathcal{I}$ REMEMBER OUR FIRST WEEK in the Tooele sixth ward. The Primary organizations in several wards in the stake were floundering. Our former twelfth ward had well over one hundred Primary-age children. Our houseful of children, bordering the sixth ward, was a logical moving target. My Church activity didn't change the fact that my heart was still in the old ward. My attitude didn't soften through two meetings, and sitting in Relief Society didn't help matters. Everyone seemed friendly enough, but I still didn't want to be there. Looking around, I spotted a few familiar faces. One new face particularly caught my attention. I looked at Alice, her stark features advertising her age, and thought how plain she appeared. I chastised myself for my thoughts and tried to concentrate on the lesson. Little did I suspect what a sermon Alice was going to preach to me in the months to come.

Several months after the ward switch, I still struggled with the move. I had made some friends and chided myself that people had become such a big part of my Sunday worship. My calling in the Church didn't help my situation. I was in a stake position, and that took me away from some meetings and kept me away from ward callings that would have built closeness through more association.

I should have been more careful about the phrasing of my request, but I was getting desperate. I prayed, "Please, Heavenly Father, I need to be shown a way to become close to sisters in my new ward." Heavenly Father must have a sense of humor. I could almost see him quietly smile as he said, "Happy to oblige," and inspired our bishop to call me as the new ward Relief Society president.

I accepted the call, and waited until I got into the car to become hysterical. My oldest daughter, Michelle, intercepted me as I came into the house. I blubbered, "How can I be Relief Society president? I've never even really been to Relief Society. I'm a Primary person. Everyone there is older than I am. They will never accept a twelfth ward transplant." I pictured an uncontrolled outburst of "you've got to be kidding" laughter as my name was read, followed by stifled gasps as they realized the bishop was serious. Michelle read me her favorite scripture about trusting in the Lord. I was quietly sustained in sacrament meeting, and went to the bishop's office to be set apart following the three-hour block.

I remember only a portion of the blessing: "Sister Molgard, I bless you with unconditional love for the sisters of the Tooele sixth ward." I felt a warm flood of love spread from my head down to my toes. The ward sisters were immediately mine.

I was soon in the middle of the flurry of the position. Thankfully, I had wonderful counselors, and Alice was retained as the sister in charge of compassionate service. In addition to helping me with every task of charity and service (she had been Relief Society president before, so she knew the ropes), her name kept cropping up in visit after visit that I made to the homes of the sisters. Once we asked a sister who was just home from the hospital if we could provide dinner for the evening. "No, thank you, Alice brought us some soup for this evening," was her quick reply. A sister who was on oxygen and unable to leave her home answered similarly: "Don't worry, Alice has been coming over to help, and I'm nicely situated." I was almost half her age, but I was struggling to come close to matching the example Alice was showing me.

After two years of service with me (and many years previous to my calling), Alice asked to be released. She was more than eighty years old and was getting weary. We quietly arranged to have her family and friends come to a special surprise homemaking night where we honored her years of service. I looked over at Alice, surrounded by her family, and saw an angelic glow radiate from her countenance. I thought, "Alice Harrison has to be one of our father's most beautiful daughters." How could the measurement so drastically change? Was I using a different yardstick for my standard?

Cooks have to use standard measuring cups and spoons. Any recipe you follow has been tested with standard equipment and the final result will be disastrous if you try measuring with other equipment. The standard works are the standard against which all truth is measured. Satan's yardstick measures such things as beauty and wealth, educational accolades, and worldly acclaim. It measures everything that has temporal worth—things that dissolve in eternity. Satan wants to make sure every one of us has his glittering yardstick. It is the special present he gives to us on our eighth birthday. His gift is too bulky to hold with one hand, necessitating putting down, then turning away from, the Savior's true standard of measurement. Sister Barbara Smith likens our worldly exchange to an old familiar story:

> Many of you remember the story of Aladdin and his wondrous lamp. It was old and tarnished, but had the magical power to make his every wish come true. One day someone realized the power within the lamp and conceived of a way to obtain it. He dressed as a peddler, walked by Aladdin's home calling out in a loud voice, "New lamps for old, new lamps for old!" Tempted by the appealing offer, Aladdin's wife seized the opportunity and chose to trade the old lamp for a new lamp of momentary brilliance ("New Lamps for Old," *Ensign*, Apr. 1976, p. 67).

Satan's yardstick is brilliant and attracts attention. Despite the fact that we don't have a yardstick of our own until the age of eight, those of others have already begun to shape our lives. Worldly competition begins at birth. Did your mother have the longest, most difficult labor? Were you the most adorable, biggest, tiniest, longest, most intelligent, most treasured baby ever born? Comparatively speaking, how fast did you learn to stand up, crawl, say your first word, and cut your first tooth?

When you started kindergarten, were you so smart you started early? Were you reading before everyone else? Did you have the nicest clothes, coordinated with your socks and hair decorations? Did you have the biggest box of crayons carried in a backpack that beat everyone else's hands down? By the time we are teenagers, we have been taught that to be of value a boy must be successful in sports and a girl must look like a fashion model. With that background, how simple it becomes to pick up Satan's yardstick and try to look for happiness in outdoing those around us.

Satan's yardstick versus the Savior's yardstick. The words are the same and that is the basis for Satan's work. His domain tries to mimic the Savior's domain. There is always a flip side to every good thing.

Satan even says he is the god of this world. He even had the audacity to offer it to the Savior: "Again, the devil taketh him up into an exceeding high mountain, and sheweth him all the kingdoms of the world, and the glory of them. And saith unto him, All these things will I give thee, if thou wilt fall down and worship me" (Matthew 4:8-9).

The Savior had created worlds without end, including our world. Satan was trying to give Christ what was already his through the Father. (Similar to your daughter loaning you your sweater that she borrowed from your closet the week before.) All that He has can be ours: "Lift up your hearts and be glad, for I am in your midst, and am your advocate with the Father; and it is his good will to give you the kingdom" (D&C 29:5).

The difference between the world Satan has to offer us and the world the Savior has to offer us is eternity. Satan's world comprises the power, riches, and glory of today, all of which will be destroyed at the end of the world (see D&C 19:3). Elder M. Russell Ballard said, "We must govern our actions every day with our future in mind. One of Satan's clever tactics is to tempt us to concentrate on the present and ignore the future" ("Purity Precedes Power," *Ensign*, Nov. 1990, p. 36). The Savior's world comprises the power, riches, and glory of eternity. He and his prophets normally speak in eternal terms; for example, the words "about to come to pass," "soon," "but a moment," and "quickly" are eternal terms and have no relevance in our present time period. That is the reason Satan can so quickly and effectively entice us with the things of the world. They can be seen and had now—seemingly without a price.

In our search for happiness, we are often deceived by thinking eternal happiness is the same as fun. David O. McKay provided us with some guidelines to use when seeking happiness.

> *Obedience to the principles of the gospel brings happiness,* and happiness is what all men seek. Indeed, the Prophet Joseph Smith said that "Happiness is the object and design of our existence, and will be the end thereof"—and this is important—"if we pursue the path that leads to it." As an end in itself, happiness is never found; it comes incidentally. Note: "It will be the end thereof *if we follow the path that leads to it,* and this path is *virtue, uprightness, faithfulness, holiness, and keeping all the commandments of God.*" (*Teachings of the Prophet Joseph Smith,* pp. 255-256.) "Happiness consists not of *having,* but of *being*—not of *possessing,* but of *enjoying.* It is a warm glow of the heart at peace with itself. A martyr at the stake may have happiness that a king on his throne might envy. Man is the creator of his own happiness. It is the aroma of life lived in harmony with high ideals. For what a man *has* he may be dependent upon others; what he *is* rests with him alone. What he obtains in life is but *acquisition;* what he attains is true *growth.*"
>
> William George Jordan continues: "The basis of happiness is the love of something outside itself. Search every instance of happiness in the world, and you will find, when all the

incidental features are eliminated, there is always the constant, unchangeable element of love—love of parent for child; love of man and woman for each other (husband and wife); love of humanity in some form, or a great life work into which the individual throws all his energies" (in Conference Report, Oct. 1955, p. 8).

I believe the true happiness we find living the gospel can be intermittently tainted by measuring ourselves with Satan's yardstick. Several years ago I had found true happiness in a home blessed with a worthy husband and six children under the age of nine. Everything would have been perfect had I been allowed to live with my family on a deserted island. I knew the things that were eternally important, but my ideal world kept bumping up against the outside world. My immaturity prompted me to put an invisible hook on my doorpost where the Savior's yardstick would be exchanged for Satan's as I left my home. Consequently, I spent an exorbitant amount of time using Satan's yardstick to measure myself against others.

We seemed to be on the lowest rung of an affluent ward ladder. Our pinewood derby cars were made by our sons and never compared to the sleek, shop-carved and body-shop-painted cars of other boys. I dreaded the days visiting teachers might see my less-than-perfect home. My clothes weren't as nice, my home wasn't as fancy, my body wasn't as shapely, and my children didn't always look or act perfect. I lived in dread that someone would discover something flawed here or less-than-perfect there, and I would become the newest "can you believe, she . . ." victim. One day I was reading about Lehi's dream:

> And after they had partaken of the fruit of the tree they did cast their eyes about as if they were ashamed.
> And I also cast my eyes round about, and beheld, on the other side of the river of water, a great and spacious building; and it stood as it were in the air, high above the earth.
> And it was filled with people, both old and young, both

male and female; and their manner of dress was exceedingly fine; and they were in the attitude of mocking and pointing their fingers toward those who had come at and were partaking of the fruit (1 Nephi 8:25–27).

As I read I distinctly heard a quiet voice whisper, "You are living your life around what the people in the high and spacious building might think of you." The truth of that statement hit me full force. I had thought I was safe because I had held tightly to the truth and had partaken of the glorious fruit of the tree. However, my path towards exaltation was slow and treacherous because of my need to constantly glance at the large and spacious building. I had allowed pride to waste my time and energy, rob me of happiness, and slow my progress. I learned, as Elder Neal A. Maxwell explained, "Playing to the gallery in all its forms involves a wearying regimen. We cannot finally be concerned about pleasing Him if we are too concerned about pleasing *them*. Besides, playing to the roar of the crowd, be it a few peers or an imagined multitude, ends as an empty exercise. One realizes finally that he is in the wrong theater" (*We Will Prove Them Herewith* [Salt Lake City: Deseret Book Co., 1982], p. 104).

I vowed to ignore my perceived tauntings, discard Satan's yardstick that I had used to measure me against everyone else (and my worldly stuff against their worldly stuff), and concentrate on keeping my eyes and my heart on the things of eternal importance. I made a conscious decision to "lay aside the things of this world, and seek for the things of a better" (D&C 25:10). For me, recognition that I was in the wrong theater, and using the wrong yardstick, was a huge step in finding my present peace and happiness.

Eliminating worldly pride from our lives is difficult. We need to check our feelings every step of the way. Is physical beauty or worldly accolades the measure you use in judging yourself or others? Elder Neal A. Maxwell gives us food for thought when he suggests, "Think for a moment how different it would be if people took on that physical appearance which would reflect distinctly how well they are doing spiritually. . . . Under such telling circumstances—when the outer person reflected the inner person—whom would we applaud? And who would really deserve out pity?" (*All These Things Shall Give Thee Experience* [Salt Lake City: Deseret Book Co., 1979], p. 61).

If you have pride in your accomplishments, is it because of your own personal growth or because you have done better than others? When your children excel, do you point out their individual growth, or gloat while you look at the children they bested and pat yourself on the back because your children are advertising your fine parenting abilities? Anne Osborne Poelman shares a wonderful example:

> Winning itself must, of course, be viewed from an eternal perspective. All too often we yearn for the praise and prize of being first rather than the much more important process of completing the task itself. A much beloved, oft-repeated story in our family is about my mother. As a child she was a very capable, successful competitive swimmer. One day my grandfather brought several friends to watch her race in a particularly important meet. One of his friends, caught up in the enthusiasm of the competition, exclaimed, "Jeannie, if you win I'll give you fifty cents." My grandfather put his arm around her shoulders and quietly said, "Jeannie, if you *lose* and are the first one to congratulate the winner I'll give you fifty cents." Nearly fifty years later I'm sure my mother can't remember whether she won that particular race or not. But our grandfather's wisdom and proper perspective became guidelines for his future generations. Do your best, win when and if possible, but keep all things in proper perspective ("Balance: The Joy of Perspective," *LDS Women's Treasury* [Salt Lake City: Deseret Book Co., 1997], p. 115).

Do you accept a call thinking how wonderful your experience and growth will be as you serve or thinking how wonderful you will appear in others' eyes in that prestigious position? (Don't worry too much about this one. Experience will teach you not to make that same mistake again.)

All these mistaken thoughts fall into the category of pride. Pride has been Satan's most effective, universal tool throughout the history of the world. No one is exempt from its destructive consequences. Satan was the premortal instigator of pride when he said, "Behold, here am *I*, send *me*, *I* will be thy son, and *I* will redeem all mankind, that one soul shall not be lost, and surely *I* will do it; wherefore give *me* thine honor" (Moses 4:1, emphasis added). The Book of Mormon is a "record of a fallen people" (D&C 20:9) who fell because "the pride of this nation, or the people of the Nephites, hath proven their destruction" (Moroni 8:27). We are warned to "beware of pride, lest [we] become as the Nephites of old" (D&C 38:39). Pride centers our thoughts on ourselves and the things of the world instead of the eternal things of God. We are cautioned: "Love not the world, neither the things that are in the world. If any man love the world, the love of the Father is not in him. For all that is in the world, the lust of the flesh, and the lust of the eyes, and the pride of life, is not of the Father, but is of the world" (1 John 2:15-16).

President Ezra Taft Benson sounded a powerful alert against pride, which he called the "universal sin, the great vice." He cautioned:

> The proud make every man their adversary by pitting their intellects, opinions, works, wealth, talents, or any other worldly measuring device against others. In the words of C. S. Lewis: "Pride gets no pleasure out of having something, only out of having more of it than the next man. . . . It is the comparison that makes you proud: the pleasure of being above the rest. Once the element of competition has gone, pride has gone." (*Mere Christianity*, New York: Macmillan, 1952, pp. 109-10.) . . .
>
> Most of us consider pride to be a sin of those on the top, such as the rich and the learned, looking down at the rest of us. (See 2 Ne. 9:42.) There is, however, a far more common ailment among us—and that is pride from the bottom looking up. It is manifest in so many ways, such as faultfinding, gossip, backbiting, murmuring, living beyond our means, envying, coveting, withholding gratitude and praise that might lift

another, and being unforgiving and jealous. . . .

Pride adversely affects all our relationships—our relationship
with God and His servants, between husband and wife, parent
and child, employer and employee, teacher and student, and all
mankind. Our degree of pride determines how we treat our God
and our brothers and sisters. Christ wants to lift us to where He
is. Do we desire to do the same for others? . . .

The antidote for pride is humility—meekness, submissive-
ness. . . .

We must cleanse the inner vessel by conquering pride. (See
Alma 6:2-4; Matt. 23:25-26.) ("Beware of Pride," *Ensign*, May
1989, pp. 4-7).

In order to understand how to conquer pride, we need to
keep an eternal perspective. Nowhere on earth does eternity link
hands with mortality more than in our holy temples. We seek the
teachings of eternity in the house of the Lord and we strive to
discard the destructive influences of Satan before entering the
temple. The peaceful setting of the temple provides us with a
clear view of what the world would look like if everyone set aside
Satan's yardstick and clung tightly to the Savior's. The things of
importance in our life are highlighted in the temple. Answers to
questions asked by the world become totally immaterial as you
walk through the doors and clothe yourself with humility.

What is your yearly income? A millionaire stands equal next
to a migrant worker. How tall are you? A professional basketball
player stands as an equal next to a petite new bride. How much
do you weigh and how many times have you yo-yoed to your
highest and lowest weights? What accolades did you receive in
high school? What position did you play, and for what team? Is
your hair color and curl natural? How many pairs of shoes do you
have in your closet, and where did you buy them? Are you married, single, divorced, or separated? How many children do you
have? Can you trace your genealogy back to the handcart pio-
neers? The blind man is as effective as the sister who has always
prided herself with 20/20 vision. A hand gnarled with age,

young and well manicured, or obviously missing at the end of a stump acknowledges covenants with the same effectiveness.

Effectiveness as a proxy is determined by the fact that you have a mortal body and are worthy—a fact established by the signature of three witnesses: you, your bishop, and a member of the stake presidency. Nothing else matters.

My parents met Max and Gwen Higginson on December 21, 1953, in the St. Alphonsus Hospital in Boise, Idaho. It was an important date for both couples. That day Gwen gave birth to a son, and my mother had me. They still keep in touch.

Seven years after we were born, the Higginsons had a special Down's syndrome son named Brent. Brent seemed to bring a touch of heaven into their home. He had difficulty learning to speak, but even when he was tiny he made it known that he wanted to go inside the temple. Gwen says whenever they would have an opportunity to go through a session at a temple, they would make arrangements for someone to watch Brent. They would let him see the temple, explain to him that someone like a grandma would be taking care of him when they went there. He would cry, "No, me in—not grandma. Please, me in." They would tell him maybe he could go in some day, but he wasn't quite big enough yet.

Brent's eighth year came and went without baptism. There was no need. Bruce R. McConkie explains:

> When a child reaches the age at which he has sufficient mental, spiritual, and physical maturity to be held accountable before God for his acts, he is said to have arrived at the *years of accountability*. He then knows right from wrong and can exercise his agency to do good or evil. . . .
> . . . Children who develop normally become accountable "when eight years old" (D. & C. 68:27), and they are then subject to the law of baptism. Obviously if children or adults do not develop mentally to the point where they know right from wrong and have the normal intellect of an accountable person, they never arrive at the years of accountability no matter how

many actual years they may live. Such persons, though they may be adults, are without the law, cannot repent, are under no condemnation, "and unto such baptism availeth nothing." (Moroni 8:22.) Because they have no "understanding" it remains for the Lord "to do according as it is written" concerning them (D. & C. 29:48–50), that is, save them through the power of his redemptive sacrifice. (Moroni 8:22.) (*Mormon Doctrine* [Salt Lake City: Bookcraft, 1979], pp. 852–53).

When Brent was fourteen, his brother was serving a mission and kept writing about all of the people who were being baptized. Brent became adamant about his desire to be baptized. Following his baptism, Brent began asking when he could be a deacon. Soon he was a deacon, and many commented at how proud he was to pass the sacrament.

In 1985 the Boise Idaho Temple was completed, just two and a half miles from Brent's home. His parents, Max and Gwen, would go through the temple regularly. By this time, Brent was twenty-four and was old enough to take care of himself. He would say, "Don't worry, I be good" and then would sit in the temple waiting room, listening to tapes of scripture stories and following along in the books while his parents participated in a session. The waiting room, however, didn't satisfy his desire to go through the temple. He seemed to be the epitome of Elder Neal A. Maxwell's saying, "True disciples are meek but very determined" ("The Pathway of Discipleship," *Ensign*, Sept. 1998, p. 8). Gwen said, "He launched a campaign that nearly drove the bishop crazy." Finally, toward the end of 1985, the bishop called them in and said, "I guess you know how much Brent desires to go through the temple. I've spoken with the stake president, and we have fasted and prayed about it. We agree that he can be made an elder and go through the temple for his endowment."

Brent received his own endowment and then desired to stand as proxy for others. After he had been several times, he was still struggling with a difficult part of the endowment. "I want to do that part better," he told his mom.

Gwen remembers explaining, "You know Brent, there is someone who can help you to do that." He quietly thought about it, then his face lit up as he understood. "I know," he responded, "Jesus can!"

That was on a Friday and Brent wouldn't be returning to the temple again until Tuesday. "Every time I saw him that entire weekend, he was on his knees asking for help," said Gwen. "The following Tuesday, it was like the heavens poured in blessings and Brent was able to do it."

Brent began going to the temple three times per week and now spends eight hours daily, five days per week acting as a proxy for fourteen endowments each week. A visiting authority recently said, "Brent Higginson has now endowed two stakes worth of souls, standing as proxy for over 4,800 endowments." Gwen smiles as she relates, "It's hard to talk Brent into going with us to visit our other children because he doesn't want to get behind in his temple work. We'll tell him about our intentions three weeks in advance so he has time to get used to the idea. He'll say, 'I know Mom, family first—but I love the temple!' "

What a blessing the temple has been to Brent, and what a blessing he has been in his thirty-nine years to his family, ward, stake, and his large circle of friends at the temple. He often spots them on shopping trips and runs to put his arms around them. As long as he is in the temple, nothing in his life is negative. Nothing of the world penetrates his days. When he sees any type of contention outside the temple, he doesn't understand. "Why would they do that? That wouldn't make Jesus happy." Brent Higginson has lived to be able to echo the words of our Savior, "In the world ye shall have tribulation: but be of good cheer; I have overcome the world" (John 16:33).

Our Divine
Armor of Protection

*T*HE WEEK AFTER FINISHING MY junior year at Box Elder High School in Brigham City, Utah, I was expecting a phone call. I had taken the courses necessary to become a life-guard and swimming instructor in the public pool and was sort of hanging around the house hoping for a call offering me the position. Sure enough, the phone rang and Mrs. Burt's deep, thundering voice congratulated me on my new employment.

The following day, my sister Vicki drove me to the pool at noon. I wore my swimming suit and a terry cloth coverup, but couldn't see any reason to wear shoes. Vicki was letting me out at the door and would pick me up at five o'clock that evening. I walked in and went behind the counter searching for Mrs. Burt. She spotted me and bellowed, "What are you doing behind the counter!" I explained that I had talked to her on the phone the day before and she had told me to report at noon. I uncomfort-ably endured her drill sergeant evaluation as she looked me up and down and then proclaimed, "You will never do. I hadn't real-ized you were so little. I'll have to find someone else." With that, she dismissed me.

You have to remember that this was 1970, a time when chil-dren were raised to be silent—even if they disagreed with an adult. I didn't say a word, but my silent inward dialogue was

121

rampant. "Just because I'm little doesn't mean I'm weak. You should have seen me the last day of my lifesaving class. I had to save Randy Summerville to pass! He was like trying to save the Incredible Hulk. He didn't scrimp at all in his panicky, dramatic struggle of drowning, in fact, he nearly drowned me, but I knew when I got him out of the pool that I could save anyone who dared try to drown on my shift!"

There I stood, my smothered excitement and indignation threatening to spill out of my eyes. There was no way I was going to let Mrs. Burt see me cry, so calling my sister on the phone was out of the question. It was a mile walk home and I hoofed it, bare feet and all, crying for my hurt feelings and hurt feet as I arrived home. Trying to stifle my sobs, I sat down to evaluate the damage. My poor feet had previously only seen the light of day inside the house. Mom always insisted that we wear shoes whenever we were outside. They were covered with inch-wide throbbing blisters.

Two weeks later, Mrs. Burt called again. She explained that they had enough lifeguards but they were short on instructors. Would I be interested in teaching the pollywog classes? I jumped at the chance and within a couple weeks, was also allowed to be a lifeguard.

I had the job I wanted, but the lifeguard job presented new problems. My Scandinavian ancestry gave me enviable blonde hair but didn't leave me anything to brag about in the skin department. Sunscreen hadn't been invented yet so we made do with baby oil (which intensified the sun's rays) and zinc oxide ointment. I quickly learned that a nose covered in bright white zinc oxide was preferable to a blistered one, and I loved my ever-whitening hair. The rest of my skin was a nightmare. I sat up on the lifeguard stand and fried the summer away. Many a morning, I'd wake up to my long hair sticking to the popped blisters on my back.

A marriage and three and a half children later, I made a preliminary trip, along with my husband, to Florida to find a home. We stayed with our soon-to-be stake president, President Moody, and his family. One day we were invited by the Moody's to share a lunch at the beach and spend the afternoon enjoying the sun and water. I had borrowed a maternity swimsuit from my sister-in-law, so I was set for the day. Lavinia Moody offered me a new product called sunscreen. I patiently tried to explain to her that nothing worked on my skin, but she insisted it worked so I put some on my hand and did an obligatory swipe across my unprotected skin. Several hours later, back at the Moody's, I emerged from my shower, glanced in the mirror and noticed some white stripes and smears in the middle of my sunburned skin. Upon further investigation I discovered I had fingermarks everywhere I had swiped the sunscreen. There was no way the dress I had brought would cover it up, so I sheepishly went to Lavinia and confessed my transgression. She had given me all the protection my skin needed and I hadn't used it.

Latter-day Saint sisters often walk around spiritually barefoot and without protective spiritual sunscreen. Our Savior and our Heavenly Father offer a protective screen. Its use and application depend on us. We must take the time to cover ourselves with protection but sometimes our hurry-scurry lives encourage only half-hearted swipes here and there. If we allow Satan access to our unprotected spirit, we will, at the very least, waste a lot of precious time battling his advances and healing our wounds. Our time is priceless. We live in the evening of the final dispensation of the fulness of times as a few covenant daughters of Heavenly Father.

Nephi saw in vision the Church of the Lamb of God in our day. Because of wickedness "its numbers were few," and "their dominions upon the face of the earth were small" (1 Nephi 4:12). He told of the strength of the forces of evil: "And it came to pass that I beheld that the great mother of abominations did gather together multitudes upon the face of all the earth, among all the nations of the Gentiles, to fight against the Lamb of God" (1 Nephi 14:13).

Nephi also saw how we would be armed and protected for this great, latter-day battle: "And it came to pass that I, Nephi, beheld the power of the Lamb of God, that it descended upon the saints of the church of the Lamb, and upon the covenant people of the Lord, who were scattered upon all the face of the earth; and they were armed with righteousness and with the power of God in great glory" (1 Nephi 14:14).

The power of the Lamb of God gives us a full suit of armor to fight the forces of evil during our personal battles. His shields consist of:

1. Learning how to access the power and protection of the Holy Ghost through effective two-way communication with Heavenly Father. This line-by-line process consists of effective prayers, scripture study, and pondering in addition to feeling, recording, and obeying spiritual impressions. Following the prophet also promises divine protection.

2. Recognizing that the weak spots in our armor will be where the adversary places his most effective attacks. Successfully overcoming our weaknesses leads to strong shields of protection. Renewing our covenants weekly allows us to access powerful protection.

3. Knowing that Satan can also attack us where we think we are strong, through our greatest talents and spiritual gifts.

4. Claiming the full power of the temple and righteously clothing ourselves in the armor worn by covenant men and women.

When young David was preparing to face his enemy, Goliath of Gath, King Saul gave him his armor and a helmet. It took David only a few steps to realize that his safety was going to be jeopardized if he continued to clank along in armor that didn't fit and that he didn't know how to use effectively. Our gift of the Holy Ghost covers us with a steel sheet of protection if we learn how to use it. Brigham Young lamented, "[We] may have the Spirit of the Lord to . . . direct [us] . . . I am satisfied, however, that in this respect, we live far beneath our privileges" (*Deseret News* Semi-Weekly, 3 Dec. 1867, p. 2).

Sister Sheri L. Dew, second counselor in the Relief Society general presidency, further enlightened us by saying:

Is it possible that in this twilight season of the dispensation of the fulness of times, when Satan and his minions roam the earth inspiring deceit, discouragement, and despair, that we who have been armed with the most potent antidote on earth—the gift of the Holy Ghost—don't always fully partake of that gift? Are we guilty of spiritually just "getting by" and not accessing the power and protection within our reach? Are we satisfied with far less than the Lord is willing to give us, essentially opting to go it alone here rather than partner with the Divine?

This Church is a church of revelation. Our challenge is not one of getting the Lord to speak to us. Our problem is hearing what He has to say. He has promised, "As often as thou hast inquired thou hast received instruction of my Spirit" (D&C 6:14).

It is vital that we, the sisters of Relief Society, learn to hear the voice of the Lord. Yet I worry that too often we fail to seek the guidance of the Spirit. Perhaps we don't know how and haven't made it a priority to learn. Or we're so aware of our personal failings that we don't feel worthy, don't really believe the Lord will talk to *us,* and therefore don't seek revelation. Or we've allowed the distractions and pace of our lives to crowd out the Spirit. What a tragedy! For the Holy Ghost blesses us with optimism and wisdom at times of challenge that we simply cannot muster on our own. . . . Sisters, we can't afford *not* to seek the things of the Spirit! There is too much at stake. Too many people are depending on us as mothers, as sisters, leaders, and friends. A woman led by the Lord knows where to turn for answers and for peace. She can make difficult decisions and face problems with confidence because she takes her counsel from the Spirit, and from her leaders who are also guided by the Spirit.

Our responsibility, therefore, is to learn to hear the voice of the Lord ("We Are Not Alone," *Ensign,* Nov. 1998, pp. 95–96).

Hearing the voice of the Lord begins on our side of the veil with prayer. In the Book of Mormon Laman and Lemuel were full of contention because they couldn't understand their father's vision. Nephi asks, "Have ye inquired of the Lord?" (1 Nephi 15:8) and they answer, "We have not" (v. 9). We won't have any more success finding answers than Laman and Lemuel did if we don't initiate the conversation.

All of our prayers, however, will not be of the same length or intensity. In addition to our regular prayers, we need to find an "intense prayer" time during the day. Some of you are morning people and some of you are night people and some fit in the middle somewhere. My husband bounds out of bed at 4:15 most mornings. His battery is fully charged and he's happy and excited about life. I find that attitude hard to relate to. The bed grabs me in the morning and hangs on. I wrestle with it and finally succeed in getting myself out of bed about 5:30 A.M. It's usually the hardest thing I do all day. Once I'm up, things are in a rush. I used to try to have my morning prayers as soon as I got up or I'd forget. They were at best a rushed list interrupted by thoughts of other things I needed to get done.

At night, both Max and I are wrung out from all we have done during the day. Heavenly Father understands our earthly limitations. If we are exhausted, a short prayer is perfectly acceptable. For those of you whose battery begins to charge as the evening goes on, your intense prayer time can be set at night.

You may have noticed that I don't do exceptionally well first thing in the morning, or in the evening. However, after school starts in the morning, a friend and I go walking for an hour, I come home and take a shower and get ready for the day and that's when I find I'm awake and alone. Those are two prime prerequisites for your intense prayer time. Did I see you young mothers roll your eyes? Did I hear you say, "awake would be nice and alone is impossible"? I really don't live in a bubble. I remember trying to say my prayers alone as a mother of six little ones. I'd kneel down by my bed and someone would jump on my back. I'd go into the bathroom and shut the door and someone would knock and demand attention. Looking back, I think I could have found one intense prayer time during the day if it didn't have to be first thing in the morning or last thing at night. A favorable possibility for you would be trading a half hour of watching children for prayer, pondering, and scripture reading time with a spouse or friend. I promise it will reap enormous benefits effecting the rest of your day.

Several steps will increase the power and effectiveness of your prayers. I have spent years praying and Heavenly Father has spent years of listening to my prayers that get started and wander off into a related tangent. I'd have to constantly apologize and bring myself back on track. The solution was simple, but powerful. The Doctrine and Covenants says, "And again, I command thee that thou shalt pray vocally as well as in thy heart; yea, before the world as well as in secret, in public as well as in private" (19:28).

President Spencer W. Kimball reiterated: "It was a prayer, a very special prayer, which opened this whole dispensation. It began with a young man's first vocal prayer. I hope that not too many of our prayers are silent, even though when we cannot pray vocally, it is good to offer a silent prayer in our hearts and in our minds" ("We Need a Listening Ear," *Ensign*, Nov. 1979, p. 48).

Private vocal prayers keep me focused. My feelings are more intense and I am better able to convey my love and needs. When I am not alone, my private prayers are quietly whispered or at least mouthed. Just that little change has made a world of difference. Those of you who worry that Satan can hear your vocal prayers have forgotten the rule. Satan cannot tolerate light.

Listening for the promptings of the Spirit during and after prayers can result in two-way communication. Elder Richard G. Scott explains how to receive spiritual guidance:

> The Savior said, "I will tell you in your *mind* and in your *heart*, by the Holy Ghost" (D&C 8:2; italics added). . . . An impression to the *mind* is very specific.
>
> Detailed words can be heard or felt and written as though the instruction were being dictated.
>
> A communication to the *heart* is a more general impression. The Lord often begins by giving impressions. Where there is a recognition of their importance and they are obeyed, one gains

more capacity to receive more detailed instruction to the *mind*.
An impression to the heart, if followed, is fortified by a more
specific instruction to the mind.

To illustrate, Elder Scott used an example of a time he had
prayed for specific guidance and was given specific answers in a
Sunday School class he was attending:

> In this experience there came such an outpouring of per-
> sonal impressions that I felt inappropriate to record in the midst
> of a Sunday School class. In a more private location I continued
> to write the feelings that flooded into my mind, as accurately as
> possible. After each powerful impression was recorded, I pon-
> dered it, seeking to confirm that I had accurately expressed the
> feelings I had received. I then prayed, expressing to the Lord
> what I thought I had been taught by the Spirit. Feelings of peace
> confirmed the appropriateness of what I had recorded. I was
> impressed to ask if there were more I should receive. There came
> further impressions and the process was repeated until I received
> some of the most precious, specific direction that anyone could
> ever hope to obtain in this life. . . .
>   . . . We often leave the more precious personal direction of
> the Spirit unheard because we do not record and respond to the
> first promptings that come to us when the Lord chooses to
> direct us or when impressions come in response to urgent
> prayer. . . .
>   . . . We can create an appropriate environment for the Holy
> Ghost to instruct us. Spiritual communication cannot be forced.
> We must qualify ourselves and be ready to receive the Lord's
> guidance and direction when He determines to provide it (*Help-
> ing Others to Be Spiritually Led* [address given at Church Educa-
> tional System religious educators symposium, BYU, 11 Aug.
> 1998], pp. 3–4, 11–12).

After hearing Elder Scott speak about receiving spiritual
impressions, I found a notebook and began writing down
impressions. Impressions can come any time, but for me they

most often come during Church, during my special prayer time, during scripture study, and while I ponder. My very best pondering time is before I get up in the morning. All is quiet and I hold still long enough to receive impressions. Elder Boyd K. Packer explained how this setting boosts our communication: "Inspiration comes more easily in peaceful settings. Such words as *quiet, still, peaceable, Comforter* abound in the scriptures: 'Be *still*, and know that I am God.' (Ps. 46:10; italics added.) And the promise, 'You shall receive my Spirit, the Holy Ghost, even the Comforter, which shall teach you the *peaceable* things of the kingdom.' (D&C 36:2; italics added)" ("Reverence Invites Revelation," *Ensign*, Nov. 1991, p. 21).

Taking time to ponder allows important whisperings to settle in our mind long enough to capture them. Taking the time to write down our impressions, then praying to make sure we understood correctly and asking if there is anything else will increase our knowledge a hundredfold. The importance of writing impressions as soon as we receive them cannot be overstated. Joseph Smith and Sidney Rigdon received a vision recorded in Section 76 of the Doctrine and Covenants. Verse 19 shows how pondering is an invitation to personal revelation: "And while we meditated upon these things, the Lord touched the eyes of our understandings and they were opened, and the glory of the Lord shone round about."

In order to be able to remember what they had learned, they were commanded at the end of the vision to "write while we were yet in the Spirit" (D&C 76:113).

At the conclusion of a blessing of any kind, write what you can remember and then ponder, pray, and write some more. Sacred experiences written down following the same pattern can blossom into powerful spiritual experiences. Always keep in mind that you, as a daughter of your Heavenly Father, can be a mighty force for good as you access spiritual gifts, line upon line, precept upon precept. Elder Bruce R. McConkie affirmed that women have, from the beginning, been entitled to impressive spiritual endowments. He said:

Where spiritual things are concerned, as pertaining to all the gifts of the Spirit, with reference to the receipt of revelation, the gaining of testimonies, the seeing of visions, in all matters that pertain to godliness and holiness and which are brought to pass as a result of personal righteousness—in all these things men and women stand in a position of absolute equality before the Lord (Quoted by Carolyn J. Rasmus, "Mormon Women: A Convert's Perspective," *Ensign*, Aug. 1980, p. 70).

Sister Sheri Dew reminds us of the importance of linking prayer and pondering with scripture study: "Some of the clearest promptings I have ever received have come while being immersed in the scriptures. They are a conduit for revelation. They teach us the language of the Spirit" ("We Are Not Alone," *Ensign*, Nov. 1998, p. 96).

The most recent editions of the scriptures offer wonderful resources that I could have used those many years ago when I was lost in the scriptures. Now, if I have a question, I check the footnotes, the Bible Dictionary, Topical Guide, and Index for explanations. I type quotes that explain scriptures, put a little glue on the edge, and paste them in my scriptures for future reference. When someone says something that clarifies a scripture, I jot it in the margins.

Our scripture study must be coupled with prayer and pondering. Otherwise, we won't be able to understand the scriptures. Nephi promises:

Wherefore, I said unto you, feast upon the words of Christ; for behold, the words of Christ will tell you all things what ye should do.

Wherefore, now after I have spoken these words, if ye cannot understand them it will be because ye ask not, neither do ye knock; wherefore, ye are not brought into the light, but must perish in the dark.

For behold, again I say unto you that if ye will enter in by the way, and receive the Holy Ghost, it will show unto you all things what ye should do (2 Nephi 32:3–5).

Another wonderful source of scriptural clarifications comes from the Brethren during general conference. They use an abundance of scriptures, and scouring the talks with my scriptures in the weeks following conference helps to extend that special conference feeling. Brother Calvin Stephens was the tour director for a Church history tour this summer. He suggested listening to general conference then, after obtaining a written copy of the talks, gleaning scriptural understanding that you can call upon later in the following way:

1. Get a 3" x 5" card for each scriptural reference.
2. Put the scriptural reference, name of author, and Conference Report or *Ensign* reference on the card.
3. Write or put a copy of the quote on the card.
4. Write an abbreviation of the quote in your scriptures.
5. Put the 3" x 5" cards in order according to scripture reference in a box.

This idea is a wonderful way to expand and retain an understanding of the scriptures.

Our prophet is on the front lines of our spiritual war. He can see when trouble is approaching. Giving "heed unto all his words and commandments" brings the following promise of divine protection: "For by doing these things the gates of hell shall not prevail against you; yea, and the Lord God will disperse the powers of darkness from before you, and cause the heavens to shake for your good and his name's glory" (D&C 21:4, 6).

Acknowledging human weakness and how quickly our memories could forget baptismal and temple covenants, Jesus gave us the sacrament. Interestingly enough, he instituted it during the Passover, the commemoration of the occasion when the firstborn were "passed over" if their covenant parents were obedient and smeared blood on their doorposts. "How fitting it was during the observance of this ancient covenant of protection that Jesus should institute the emblems of the new covenant of safety—the emblems of his own body and blood" (Howard W. Hunter, "His

Final Hours," *Ensign*, May 1974, p. 18). Every week we are reminded of the protection given to us at baptism if we are willing to always remember our Savior. Always having his Spirit to be with us is a strong shield of protection against Satan. Joseph Fielding Smith cautioned us against the consequences of neglecting the power of the sacrament:

> No member of the Church can fail to make this covenant and renew it week by week, and retain the Spirit of the Lord. The Sacrament meeting of the Church is the most important meeting which we have, and is sadly neglected by many members. We go to this service, if we understand the purpose of it, not primarily to hear someone speak, important though that may be, but first, and most important, to renew this covenant with our Father in heaven in the name of Jesus Christ. Those who persist in their absence from this service will eventually lose the Spirit and if they do not repent will eventually find themselves denying the faith (*Church History and Modern Revelation* [Salt Lake City: The Council of the Twelve Apostles of The Church of Jesus Christ of Latter-Day Saints, 1946], pp. 122–23).

Elder Melvin J. Ballard explained:

> No man goes away from this Church and becomes an apostate in a week or in a month. It is a slow process. The one thing that would make for the safety of every man and woman would be to appear at the sacrament table every Sabbath day. We would not get very far away in one week—not so far away that, by the process of self-investigation, we could not rectify the wrongs we may have done. If we should refrain from partaking of the sacrament, condemned by ourselves as unworthy to receive these emblems, we could not endure that long, and we would soon, I am sure, have the spirit of repentance. The road to the sacrament table is the path of safety for Latter-day Saints (*Melvin J. Ballard: Crusader for Righteousness* [Salt Lake City: Bookcraft, 1966], p. 134).

Satan recognizes our spiritual endowments, and sends armies to counteract them. He knows where to find the gaps in our armor. Clyde J. Williams, a professor at BYU, gives further insight when he says, "We are not capable of overcoming Satan alone. Because he remembers the premortal existence, he may know things about us that even we do not yet understand" ("A Shield Against Evil," *Ensign*, Jan. 1996, p. 32).

He knows the weak spots in our armor and will put his greatest efforts into chiseling away at and destroying that piece. My barefoot walk home from the pool didn't hurt my body. It was protected. My feet had no protection and that's where the damage was done. Harold B. Lee said:

> The most important commandment is the one you have difficulty keeping today. Now, if you have made mistakes, make today the beginning of a change of your lives. Turn from the thing that you have been doing that is wrong. The most important of all the commandments of God is that one that you are having the most difficulty keeping today. If it is one of dishonesty, if it is one of unchastity, if it is one of falsifying, not telling the truth, today is the day for you to work on that until you have been able to conquer that weakness. Put that aright and then you start on the next one that is most difficult for you to keep. That's the way to sanctify yourself by keeping the commandments of God (Devotional, Long Beach, CA, 29 Apr. 1973) (*The Teachings of Harold B. Lee,* ed. Clyde J. Williams [Salt Lake City: Bookcraft, 1996], p. 82).

There are several ways to discover your weaknesses. Heavenly Father knows your deficiencies even better than Satan. He will almost always give you cautions and recommendations pertaining to your weaknesses in your patriarchal blessing. Look for specific spiritual deficiencies as you read yours. Or ask Father in Heaven in humility which weakness of yours is of most concern to him. Follow the pattern and promised blessing of Ether 12:27: "And if [women] come unto me I will show unto them their weakness. I give unto [women] weakness that they may be humble; and my grace is sufficient for all [women] that humble themselves before me; for if they humble themselves before me, and have faith in me, then will I make weak things become strong unto them."

The Apostle Paul speaks of a "thorn in the flesh." We don't know specifically what Paul's weakness was but he recognized that its source was Satan. He sought help and understanding and was taught by the Lord that his "strength is made perfect in weakness" (see 2 Corinthians 12:7-9). Without overcoming his weakness, he would never have become the strong Apostle who used that strength in the work of the Lord.

The Lord has all of the powers and gifts that are needed (his grace is sufficient) to help us to know how to strengthen that weak part of our armor. With his help, the weak place will become a strength. Moroni prepared his people for a physical battle with the Lamanites, but the pattern and results can be the same for our spiritual battles: "And in their weakest fortifications he did place the greater number of men; and thus he did fortify and strengthen the land which was possessed by the Nephites. And thus he was preparing to support their liberty . . . and their peace, and that they might . . . maintain that which was called by their enemies the cause of Christians" (Alma 48:9-10).

Because of those preparations and fortifications in their weakest places, they were prepared for the battle. They were victorious, but beyond their victory, "behold, to [the Lamanites'] astonishment, the city of Noah, which had hitherto been a weak place, had now, by the means of Moroni, become strong, yea, even to exceed the strength of the city Ammonihah" (Alma 49:14).

A couple years after we were married, I got on my knees to visit with Heavenly Father about a weakness that was obvious to me and I knew would soon be obvious to others. I found myself married to a young bishop who loved the scriptures and was multiplying his knowledge daily as he taught seminary. I had been raised in a part-member family and had read the Book of Mormon once (speed-reading style) to get an A in seminary. That was my sum total of scripture reading experience except to memorize specific scriptures to get jewels on my green Primary bandolo. Any further attempts resulted in confusion. I didn't understand what I was reading. I didn't like the scriptures. When I finally worked up the courage to confess that fact to Heavenly Father (who, of course, knew before I confessed), I was desperate. I didn't want anyone to find out how scripturally illiterate I was. But I couldn't make myself read something I didn't understand at all and had no compelling reason to study. So I asked Heavenly Father if he could think of a way to help me to like the scriptures.

Let me give you some sage advice based on several past experiences. Be very careful what you ask for. The following week I was called to be the stake Spiritual Living teacher in Relief Society. For those too young to remember, this calling meant that I was to be the teacher who would teach the other teachers, and Sister Raymond (our stake president's wife who got up early to study her scriptures every morning) was one of those teachers. My bucket of tears ranneth over! How could I teach Sister Raymond when I didn't know anything? Max assured me that he would help and he spoon-fed me every lesson I gave. I'm sure Sister Raymond didn't learn much, but what I learned planted a seed of love for the scriptures that has since fully blossomed. I learned the truth of the saying "to know them is to love them." My long-ago weakness is now a firmly welded strength to my armor.

Elder Dallin H. Oaks sounds a voice of warning that our strengths can also be distorted to become weaknesses.

Those who engage in self-congratulation over a supposed strength have lost the protection of humility and are vulnerable to Satan's using that strength to produce their downfall. In contrast, if we are humble and teachable, hearkening to the commandments of God, the counsel of his leaders, and the promptings of his Spirit, we can be guided in how to use our spiritual gifts, our accomplishments, and all of our other strengths for righteousness. And we can be guided in how to avoid Satan's efforts to use our strengths to cause our downfall.

In all of this, we should remember and rely on the Lord's direction and promise: "Be thou humble; and the Lord thy God shall lead thee by the hand, and give thee answer to thy prayers" (D&C 112:10) ("Our Strengths Can Become Our Downfall," *Ensign*, Oct. 1994, p. 19).

However strong the armor, full protection will not be realized until a Latter day Saint woman is "endowed with power from on high" (D&C 38:32). The opposition knows what a shield of protection worthy temple attendance offers, both for the newcomers and those who continue to fortify their shields by continuous participation. Satan has kept hundreds of righteous Latter-day Saint women away from the temple by whispering, "You're not good enough to go," "you'll never be able to pay your bills if you pay tithing," "you don't have time this week," etc. Any whisperings that are keeping you from going to the temple are lies. If, for some reason, you are not currently a temple recommend holder, make an appointment with your bishop. He holds the keys that will give you the power to overcome those things that are keeping you from going to the temple. Heavenly Father wants to give you all the temple has to offer.

Elder Carlos E. Asay, an emeritus member of the First Quorum of the Seventy and president of the Salt Lake Temple reminds us of an important piece of armor worn by both covenant men and women called the garment of the Holy Priesthood:

> It is written that "the white garment symbolizes purity and helps assure modesty, respect for the attributes of God, and, to the degree it is honored, *a token of what Paul regarded as taking upon one the whole armor of God* (Eph. 6:13; cf. D&C 27:15).
> . . . The real battles of life in our modern day will be won by those who are clad in a spiritual armor. . . . The piece of armor called the temple garment not only provides the comfort and warmth of a cloth covering, it also strengthens the wearer to resist temptation, fend off evil influences, and stand firmly for

the right ("The Temple Garment," *Ensign*, Aug. 1997, pp. 19–23).

A letter from the First Presidency dated October 10, 1988, adds, "Endowed members of the Church wear the garment as a reminder of the sacred covenants they have made with the Lord and also as a protection against temptation and evil. How it is worn is an outward expression of an inward commitment to follow the Savior."

Doctrine & Covenants 109 is the prayer given to the Prophet Joseph Smith by revelation and offered at the dedication of the temple at Kirtland, Ohio. Verse 22 gives one of the many glorious promises to those who attend the temple worthily: "And we ask thee, Holy Father, that thy servants may go forth from this house armed with thy power, and that thy name may be upon them, and thy glory be round about them, and thine angels have a charge over them."

It is a glorious vision of our protection. I particularly like the last sentence. I started doing family history work a couple years ago. The disadvantage of having a nonmember dad has turned into a wonderful addiction (most people call it the Spirit of Elijah). None of Dad's family's work had been done. They were waiting for me beyond the veil on my first trip to the Family History Library. As Melvin J. Ballard said, "They know where their records are, and . . . the spirit and influence of your dead will guide those who are interested in finding those records. If there is anywhere on the earth anything concerning them, you will find it. . . . If we have done our best and have searched and have discovered all that is available, then the day will come when God will open and part the veil, and the records . . . will be revealed" (Bryant S. Hinckley, *Sermons and Missionary Services of Melvin Joseph Ballard* [Salt Lake City: Deseret Book Co., 1949], p. 230).

I hope they weren't too disappointed at their inept descendant as they tried whispering the first time I walked past the table with the set of books entitled, *German Immigrants to America*. The second and third time I went zooming past the same table it seemed to beckon to me. Finally, when I'm sure they had received a special emergency permit to allow half the Spiekerman family to block my path and the other half to push me towards the table while shouting in my ear to go towards the book that was falling from the shelf, I listened. I think they went a little further than normally permitted, but it worked. Since that day, I have learned to pray and follow quiet promptings as we work together in the library.

One particular day I was turning the handle to a microfilm that told the story of my ancestor Maaike de Wit who married Dirk Pieck on July 15, 1818, as a young twenty-one-year-old in the Netherlands. They had a son, Mattheus, in 1819. I was quite enjoying putting the pieces together until Maaike's life started to fall apart before my eyes. Cornelia Johanna Pieck was born on September 20, 1820, and died the twenty-first of November that same year. The pattern continued with Johannes: born February 22, 1822; died November 20, 1823. And Cornelia: born July 12, 1823; died October 6, 1823. Another Cornelia: born July 19, 1824; died October 14, 1824. I found myself praying for this young mother, "Please let her keep the next one," but the tragedy was 173 years old, and it continued. Another Cornelia: born November 6, 1825; died December 6, 1825. Anna Elizabeth: born February 19, 1827; died February 27, 1827. Another Cornelia: born June 2, 1828; died May 30, 1829. Finally, Johannes was born January 25, 1830 and died April 20, 1830, just two months before Maaike's husband, Dirk, passed away. Tears streamed down my cheeks for my little Maaike who in twelve years of marriage had buried eight babies and only had one son, her firstborn, to bring a measure of comfort.

Further searching brought a happy moment when Maaike married Willem Koek in 1831. Then two more babies, Johanna in 1832 and Johannes in 1833, both buried months after their births. The final baby, another Johannes, born September 8, 1836, apparently completed their little family and survived. I thrilled when I discovered the birth of her first granddaughter, named Maaike after a grandmother who never raised a daughter of her own. A careful scan of the temple records showed her name had been forgotten and the children she lost in mortality were not a part of an eternal chain.

A full two hundred years after her birth, Maaike de Wit's name was remembered in the Salt Lake Temple when my husband spoke it as I stood proxy for her baptism. It was spoken again for her confirmation, initiatory, and endowment. On October 22, 1997, Maaike de Wit received back one precious child after another as proxies, sealer, and our Savior joined them for eternity. I left the temple that evening feeling armed with the power of service, having had a joyful glimpse into the eternities. My sheet of protection felt strong and my spirit inaccessible to anything except light. Boyd K. Packer explained that wonderful feeling: "No work is more of a protection to this Church than temple work and the genealogical research which supports it. No work is more spiritually refining. No work we do gives us more power. No work requires a higher standard of righteousness. Our labors in the temple cover us with a shield and a protection, both individually and as a people" (*The Holy Temple* [Salt Lake City: Bookcraft, 1980], p. 265).

With our full shield of protection firmly in place, the layers build upon each other until they will eventually become an impenetrable armor. Marching arm-in-arm, covenant women and covenant men are becoming a powerful army as we help establish the Kingdom of God on the earth. Through our service in the Lord's latter-day kingdom, we will gather his people. Battling the forces of evil, we will be a part of the powerful throng that will usher in that glorious Millenial day when, "because of the righteousness of his people, Satan has no power; wherefore, he cannot be loosed for the space of many years; for he hath no power over the hearts of the people, for they dwell in righteousness, and the Holy One of Israel reigneth" (1 Nephi 22:26).

With the full measure of our mortal creation completed, we will feel the arms of his love around us and hear, "Well done, good and faithful [daughter] . . . enter thou into the joy of thy lord" (Matthew 25:23).

Index